FUNDAMENTALS OF
THE PERSIAN ALPHABET

Fundamentals of the Persian Alphabet introduces complete beginners to the letters and sounds of Persian through pronunciation, basic vocabulary and phrases, conversation, and Persian culture. Students are also introduced to the distinction between the formal and informal forms of the language. As knowledge of letter–sound correspondence and phonological awareness is key to language learning, this textbook ensures learners start their learning journey with a strong foundation.

This book is divided into six lessons presenting the modern Persian alphabet in groups of mostly similarly shaped letters that will allow learners to begin blending letters and segmenting words as soon as possible to make learning easier. With the guidance of additional audio and video resources, a comprehensive Persian–English glossary, and listening, speaking, reading, and writing exercises throughout the book, students will acquire the fundamental skills and knowledge for furthering their learning of the language.

The ideal starting point for beginners, *Fundamentals of the Persian Alphabet* is designed for learners with very little or no previous knowledge of the language and is suitable for both independent and class-based study.

Shahla Adel is Teaching Associate Professor of Persian Language and Culture at the University of North Carolina at Chapel Hill, USA, as well as Visiting Associate Professor of Practice and the Persian Language Coordinator at Duke University, Durham, USA.

FUNDAMENTALS OF THE PERSIAN ALPHABET

Letters and Sounds

Shahla Adel

Routledge
Taylor & Francis Group

LONDON AND NEW YORK

Designed cover image: ugurhan / Getty Images

First published 2023
by Routledge
4 Park Square, Milton Park, Abingdon, Oxon OX14 4RN

and by Routledge
605 Third Avenue, New York, NY 10158

Routledge is an imprint of the Taylor & Francis Group, an informa business

© 2023 Shahla Adel

The right of Shahla Adel to be identified as author of this work has been asserted in accordance with sections 77 and 78 of the Copyright, Designs and Patents Act 1988.

All rights reserved. No part of this book may be reprinted or reproduced or utilised in any form or by any electronic, mechanical, or other means, now known or hereafter invented, including photocopying and recording, or in any information storage or retrieval system, without permission in writing from the publishers.

Trademark notice: Product or corporate names may be trademarks or registered trademarks, and are used only for identification and explanation without intent to infringe.

British Library Cataloguing-in-Publication Data
A catalogue record for this book is available from the British Library

ISBN: 978-1-032-12101-7 (hbk)
ISBN: 978-1-032-12100-0 (pbk)
ISBN: 978-1-003-22302-3 (ebk)

DOI: 10.4324/9781003223023

Typeset in Times New Roman
by Apex CoVantage, LLC

Access the Support Material: www.routledge.com/9781032121000

CONTENTS

Acknowledgments   ix

1   Hi! How Are You?   درس یک: سلام! چطوری؟   1

    1 The Persian Alphabet and Script 1
    2 Special Characteristics of the Persian Alphabet 2
    3 System of Transliteration of Persian Characters 5
    4 Letters 6
      A. The Letter (alef) ا *6*
      B. The Letter (be) ب *7*
      C. The Letter (pe) پ *8*
      D. The Letter (te) ت *9*
      E. The Letter (dāl) د *10*
      F. The Letter (re) ر *11*
    5 Grammar 14
      Word Stress 14
      Formal and Spoken Registers in Persian 14
    6 Listening and Conversation 14
      Greetings and Replying to Greetings 14
      Introducing Yourself 15
      Asking Others to Introduce Themselves 15
      Listening and Conversation Vocabulary 16
      Vocabulary Review Chart 17

2   Nice to Meet You!   درس دو: آشنایی و معرفی   18

    1 Letters 18
      A. The Letter (sin) س *18*
      B. The Letter (shin) ش *19*

C. *The Letter* (mim) م *21*
D. *The Letter* (nun) ن *21*
E. *The Letter* (vāv) و *25*
F. *The Letter* (ye) ى *27*
Long and Short Vowels *31*
2 Grammar *35*
Syllable Structure *35*
Personal Pronouns *36*
Important Notes about Personal Pronouns *37*
3 Listening and Conversation *38*
Morning Greetings *38*
Introducing Others *38*
Saying Goodbye *39*
Listening and Conversation Vocabulary *40*
Vocabulary Review Chart *40*

3 What's this? درس سه: این چیست؟   42

1 Letters *42*
A. *The Letter* (jim) ج *42*
B. *The Letter* (che) چ *43*
C. *The Letter* (ḥe) ح *44*
D. *The Letter* (khe) خ *45*
E. *The Letter* (ze) ز *49*
F. *The Letter* (zhe) ژ *50*
G. *The Letter* (he) ه *53*
2 Grammar *58*
Demonstrative Pronouns and Adjectives *58*
Present Tense of the Verb "To Be" بودَن *60*
Long Form of the Verb "To Be" بودَن *61*
Negative Form of the Verb "To Be" *61*
Spoken Form of "To Be" *61*
Word Order *62*
3 Listening and Conversation *63*
What Is This Called? *63*
Listening and Conversation Vocabulary *64*
Vocabulary Review Chart *65*

4 What Do You Do? درس چهار: شغل شما چیست؟   66

1 Letters *66*
A. *The Letter* (ṣād) ص *66*
B. *The Letter* (żād) ض *67*
C. *The Letter* (ṭā) ط *72*
D. *The Letter* (ẓā) ظ *72*

E. The Letter ('eyn) ع 74
F. The Letter (gheyn) غ 75
G. The Letter (lām) ل 80
2 Grammar 83
Short Form of the Verb "To Be" 83
Some Points about the Short Form of "To Be" 83
The Negation 85
Ezāfe 86
3 Listening and Conversation 87
Asking Someone What Job They Do and Talking About
    What Job You Do 87
Listening and Conversation Vocabulary 92
Vocabulary Review Chart 92

5 Where Are You From?   درس پنج: اهل کجایی؟   94

1 Letters 94
A. The Letter (fe) ف 94
B. The Letter (qāf) ق 95
C. The Letter (kāf) ک 98
D. The Letter (gāf) گ 99
2 Grammar 103
The Plural 103
Adjectival ی /-ye/ 105
3 Listening and Conversation 106
Asking Where Someone Is From 106
Listening and Conversation Vocabulary 110
Vocabulary Review Chart 111

6 Family   درس شش: خانواده   113

1 Letters 113
A. The Letter (se) ث 113
B. The Letter (zāl) ذ 114
C. The Silent /vāv/ 117
D. Tashdid ّ 119
E. Tanvin ً 120
2 Grammar 123
Pronominal Suffixes 123
The Simple Present Tense 123
Present Stem 124
The Present-Tense Verbal Endings 124
Spoken Form of the Present Tense 125
The Negation 125
The Present Tense of "To Have" 126

3 Listening and Conversation 131
Listening and Conversation Vocabulary 136
Vocabulary Review Chart 137

Glossary *138*

ACKNOWLEDGMENTS

I would like to thank the team at Routledge who have provided great support and assistance in publishing this book. I am also thankful to my students for their invaluable feedback and suggestions.

I am extremely grateful to my family, especially my daughters, who are a constant source of encouragement and inspiration.

I dedicate this book, with love and gratitude, to the memory of my parents.

Lesson 1

HI! HOW ARE YOU? درس یک: سلام! چطوری؟

In this lesson you will learn:

- The Persian Alphabet and Script
- Special Characteristics of the Persian Alphabet
- System of Transliteration of Persian Characters
- Letters

  ا د ر
  ب پ ت

- Grammar
  - Word Stress
  - Formal/Written and Informal/Spoken Persian
- Listening and Conversation
  - Greetings and Replying to Greetings
  - Introducing Yourself
  - Asking Others to Introduce Themselves

---

1 The Persian Alphabet and Script

The alphabet is a prelude to entering the original and rich Persian language. A language that, although very old, its intellectual and cultural achievement of centuries has pervaded the world. The power of the Persian language is real, and it can be boldly said that Persian is among the first languages in the world in terms of its richness of literary works in the past and present.

As language learning starts with learning the alphabet, here is a glance at the Persian alphabet, which consists of 32 letters. Listen to the audio for the names of the letters.

درس یک: سلام! چطوری؟ Hi! How Are You?

ح /he/	چ /che/	ج /jim/	ث /se/	ت /te/	پ /pe/	ب /be/	ا /alef/	
ش /shin/	س /sin/	ژ /zhe/	ز /ze/	ر /re/	ذ /zāl/	د /dāl/	خ /khe/	
ق /qāf/	ف /fe/	غ /gheyn/	ع /'eyn/	ظ /zā/	ط /tā/	ض /zād/	ص /sād/	
ی /ye/	ه /he/	و /vāv/	ن /nun/	م /mim/	ل /lām/	گ /gāf/	ک /kāf/	

2 Special Characteristics of the Persian Alphabet

Some distinctive features of the Persian alphabet and writing system are as follows:

1. The Persian alphabet is written and read from right to left and it is based on the Arabic script. Arabic has 28 letters, while Persian has four additional letters that do not exist in the Arabic language. The following chart shows these four letters:

Sound	Letter
[p]	پ
[ch]	چ
[zh]	ژ
[g]	گ

2. In Persian, letters have different shapes and can connect in different forms depending on their position in a word. The various positions of letters include the beginning, middle, or end of a word. Shapes of the letters vary when they are written in the initial, medial, or final position. The chart that follows shows the different forms of three letters from the alphabet in the initial, medial, and final positions, as well as the freestanding form.

Final Position	Medial Position	Initial Position	Sound	Freestanding Position
ﭗ	ﭙ	ﭘ	[p]	پ
ﭻ	ﭽ	ﭼ	[ch]	چ
ﻪ	ﻬ	ﻫ	[h]	ه

3. Letters have three or four different forms based on connectivity and their occurrence at the beginning, middle, or end of a word as indicated in the previous table. Most of the letters of the alphabet are two-way connectors, meaning they connect both to preceding

درس یک: سلام! چطوری؟ Hi! How Are You?   **3**

and following letters, as shown in the following example with the letter پ *[p]* in different positions:

توپ	کمپوت	پا	پیپ
[tup] ball	*[komput]* compote	*[pā]* foot	*[pip]* pipe

There are, however, seven letters of the alphabet known as one-way connectors that only connect to the following letters. These letters are

و	ژ	ز	ر	ذ	د	ا
vāv	*zhe*	*ze*	*re*	*zal*	*de*	*alef*

These seven letters have two forms, a freestanding and a connected position. Notice the letter د *[dāl]* in different positions:

پدَر	دَر
[pedar] father	*[dar]* door

4. The Persian alphabet has 23 consonants and six vowels. The three long vowels are /ā, i, u/, and depending on whether they occur in the beginning, middle, or end of the word, they have different shapes as indicated in the following chart:

Long Vowels					
At the Beginning	Sound	Example	In the Medial & Final Positions	Sound	Example
آ	*[ā]* as in *fall*	آب *[āb]* water	ا	*[ā]* as in *fall*	بابا *[bābā]* father
ای	*[i]* as in *feel*	این *[in]* this	ی / یـ	*[i]* as in *fee*	سینی *[sini]* tray
او	*[u]* as in *tooth*	او *[u]* he/she	و	*[u]* as in *tooth*	موش *[mush]* mouse

The three short vowels are /a, e, o/ and are usually not written. Instead, diacritics are used above or below a letter. Diacritics are signs that, when written, indicate a difference in pronunciation, such as (´ placed above a letter sounds *a*, ‚ placed below a letter sound *e*, and ‛ placed above a letter sound *o*). However, these vowels in the initial position are written with an *alef* (vowels are discussed in detail in Lesson 2). Here is a table with the three short vowels in different positions:

درس یک: سلام! چطوری؟ Hi! How Are You?

Short Vowels					
At the Beginning	Sound	Example	Medial & Final Positions	Sound	Example
آ	a	آسب [asb] horse	ﹷ fathe/zebar	a	مَن [man] I, me
ا	e	اسم [esm] name	ﹻ kasre/zir	e	سه [se] three
اُ	o	اُتاق [otā q] room	ﹹ zame/pish	o	شُما [shomā] you

5. There are three additional diacritics in the Persian writing system, *hamze, tashdid,* and *tanvin* (discussed in Lesson 6). It is important to note that most of the diacritics are not used in modern writing, and their occasional use is for clarity. However, two of the diacritics more likely to be seen in modern writing are *hamze* and *tanvin*.

6. In Persian, there are letters that have the same sound. For example, although letters ت /te/ and ط /tā/ are two different letters with different shapes, they both represent the same sound /t/. Other examples are listed in the table that follows.

Sounds	/t/	/s/	/h/	/gh/	/z/	/ʔ/
Letters	ت ط	س ص ث	ح ه	غ ق	ز ذ ض ظ	ع ء

7. Dots are used to distinguish letters. Oftentimes, letters with similar shapes are distinguished based on the number of dots they have, as well as whether the dots are placed above or below a letter. For example, the letter ب /be/ has one dot, ت /te/ has two, and پ /pe/ has three dots.

One-Dot Letters		Two-Dot Letters		Three-Dot Letters	
Name	Letter	Name	Letter	Name	Letter
be	ب	te	ت	pe	پ
je	ج	qāf	ق	se	ث
khe	خ			che	چ
zāl	ذ			zhe	ژ
ze	ز			shin	ش
zād	ض				
zā	ظ				

5 درس یک: سلام! چطوری؟ Hi! How Are You?

One-Dot Letters		Two-Dot Letters		Three-Dot Letters	
Name	Letter	Name	Letter	Name	Letter
gheyn	غ				
fe	ف				
nun	ن				

8. In contrast to the letters with the same sound above, there are three letters that each have several sounds. These letters are. و ، ه ، ی
9. The Persian alphabet does not have capital letters. However, letters differ in shape depending on whether the letter occurs in the beginning, middle, or end of a word, as discussed earlier.

3 System of Transliteration of Persian Characters

While you are learning the Persian alphabet and its sound system, you will also be learning and practicing greetings and short conversations. However, you might not have learned the letters needed to write the conversations earlier on; therefore, a system of transliteration of Persian becomes necessary. The transliteration system used in this book is shown in the following charts:

🎧 Consonants

Symbol & Sound	Letter	Symbol & Sound	Letter
ż	ض	b	ب
ṭ	ط	p	پ
ẓ	ظ	t	ت
ʼ	ع	s̱	ث
gh	غ	j	ج
f	ف	ch	چ
q	ق	ḥ	ح
k	ک	kh	خ
g	گ	d	د
l	ل	ẕ	ذ
m	م	r	ر
n	ن	z	ز
v	و	zh	ژ
h	ه	s	س
y	ی	sh	ش
		ṣ	ص

درس یک: سلام! چطوری؟ Hi! How Are You?

🎧 Vowels

Symbol & Sound	Short Vowel
a	‍َا
e	‍ِا
o	‍ُا

Symbol & Sound	Long Vowel
ā	آ
i	ای
u	او

🎧 **Exercise 1.** Read the following list of words using the transliteration symbols from the preceding charts.

1. tehrān	7. kordestān	13. āmrikā
2. esfehān/esfahān	8. khorāsān	14. irān
3. shirāz	9. bushehr	15. kānādā
4. tabriz	10. ābādān	16. engelis
5. rasht	11. māzandarān	17. farānse
6. mashhad	12. kermān	18. hend

4 Letters

A. The Letter (alef) ا

The first letter of the Persian Alphabet is called *alef*. This letter has two different shapes, and depending on whether it is in the freestanding position or connected to preceding letters, it is written differently. The sound of this letter as freestanding or independent in medial and final positions, as well as in the connected form is /ā/ as in the English word *fall*. In the independent position, *alef* is written from top to bottom and, in the connected position, from the bottom up.

Connected From the Right	Freestanding Position
ل	ا

📹 **Exercise 2.** Watch the video for how the shapes of the letter *alef* are written. Trace the model letter; then write your own in the space provided as you pronounce it aloud. By

7 درس یک: سلام! چطوری؟ Hi! How Are You?

tracing the model letter before writing them yourself, you will gain an awareness of finger and hand movements that will help you form the proper letter shapes.

For *alef* to sound *[ā]* as in *fall* in the beginning of a word or the initial position, it requires the diacritic symbol *madd* placed over the alef, and it is called *alef madd*.

Exercise 3. Watch the video. Trace over the model letter *alef* with *madd*, then write your own in the space provided and pronounce it aloud.

Exercise 4. Circle all the *alefs* in the following words.

آهو   باد   باران   تاب   آبی   بابا   آب

B. The Letter (be) ب

This letter is pronounced /b/ as in the English word *boy* and has four different forms depending on its position in the word (initial, medial, final, or freestanding). To write this letter, start each form from right to left, and after you are done with the body of the letter, place one dot below and close to the letter. It should be noted that in the initial position, *be* connects to any letter that follows it, but in the medial position, it can be connected from both sides. In the final position, *be* can only connect to a letter that precedes it.

Freestanding	Final	Medial	Initial
ب	ب	ب	ب

Exercise 5. Watch the video for how the shapes of the letter ب are written. Trace the model letter, and then practice writing your own in the space provided and pronounce it as you write it.

8 Hi! How Are You? ‫درس یک: سلام! چطوری؟‬

C. The Letter (pe) ‫پ‬

This letter is pronounced /p/ as in the word *pen*, and similar to the letter ‫ب‬, it has four different shapes: the initial, medial, final, and independent freestanding forms. Unlike the letter ‫ب‬ that has one dot placed below, the letter *pe* has three dots that are placed below the letter. In terms of connectivity to other letters, *pe* is similar to the letter ‫ب‬. It connects to any letter following it when it is in the initial position. It connects to previous and following letters in the medial position, and finally, it connects to any letter that precedes it in the final position.

Freestanding	Final	Medial	Initial
‫پ‬	‫ـپ‬	‫ـپـ‬	‫پـ‬

Exercise 6. Watch the video for how the shapes of the letter ‫پ‬ are written. Trace the model letter, and then practice writing your own in the space provided and pronounce it aloud.

D. The Letter ت (te)

This letter is pronounced /t/ as in *top*, and like the letters ب and پ it has four different shapes. The writing of the shapes is similar to the other two letters except that it has two dots that are placed above the letter. Also, like the letters ب and پ, letter ت is a connecting letter. It connects to any letter following it in the initial position. The medial position links it to both preceding and following letters, and in the final position, it connects to preceding letters.

Freestanding	Final	Medial	Initial
ت	ت	ـتـ	تـ

📹 **Exercise 7.** Watch the video for how the shapes of the letter ت are written. Trace the model letter, and then practice writing your own in the space provided and pronounce it aloud.

🎧 **Exercise 8.** Listen to the audio, and circle the words that you hear.

3. آت / تا	2. باب / تاب	1. آب / آپ
6. پاب / پاپ	5. پا / با	4. تات / پات
9. بابا / پاپا	8. بات / تاپ	7. تاتا / آ تا

Exercise 9. Practice joining the letters in their different shapes.

10 درس یک: سلام! چطوری؟ Hi! How Are You?

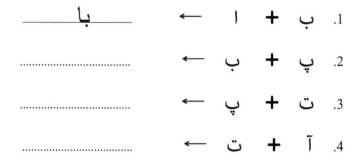

.1 ب + ا ← با _____

.2 پ + ب ← ....

.3 ت + پ ← ....

.4 آ + ت ← ....

E. The Letter (dāl) د

This letter is pronounced as /d/ in the word *dip*. Similar to *alef*, this letter is a one-way connector, which means it does not connect to following letters. Rather, it only connects to preceding letters. Letter د only has two shapes, one that is freestanding and a second one that connects to preceding letters. In writing the letter in the freestanding position, begin above the line and create an angle. To write the connected form, start with the connect part above the line, go up, and then make an angle.

Connected from the right	Freestanding Position
ـد	د

🎧 **Exercise 10.** Watch the video for how the shapes of the letter د are written. Trace the model letter, and then practice writing your own in the space provided and pronounce it aloud.

Exercise 11. Join the letters in each set to form words, and then read the words. Remember to read from right to left.

درس یک: سلام! چطوری؟ Hi! How Are You?

1. آ + ب ← آب _____
2. ب + ا + د ← ....
3. ت + ا + ب ← ....
4. د + ا + د ← ....
5. ب + ا + ب + ا ← ....
6. ا + د + ا + ب ← ....
7. ت + ا + پ ← ....
8. ا + ب + ا + د ← ....
9. ت + ا + د ← ....
10. پ + ا + پ ← ....

F. The Letter (re) ر

The letter *re* is an alveolar flap, which is similar to the /r/ sound in Spanish, as in the word *carne [karne]* meaning "meat." This letter is a one-way connector, meaning that it is similar to ا and د and does not connect to following letters. It only connects to preceding letters. In writing this letter, start above the line and draw a curved line below the line.

Connected from the right	Freestanding Position
ـر	ر

Exercise 12. Watch the video for how the shapes of the letter ر are written. Trace the model letter, and then practice writing your own in the space provided and pronounce it aloud.

درس یک: سلام! چطوری؟ Hi! How Are You?

ر ر ر

ر ر ر

🎧 **Exercise 13.** Read the following words. Remember to read from right to left.

3. بابا	2. آب	1. داد
6. تاب	5. دارا	4. آرد
9. بار	8. باد	7. آباد

🎧 **Exercise 14.** Listen to the audio, and circle the words that you hear.

3. آرد / آرت	2. تار / دار	1. باد / بات
6. تاد / تات	5. دات / داد	4. راد / رات

Exercise 15. Join the letters in each set to form words, as in the example.

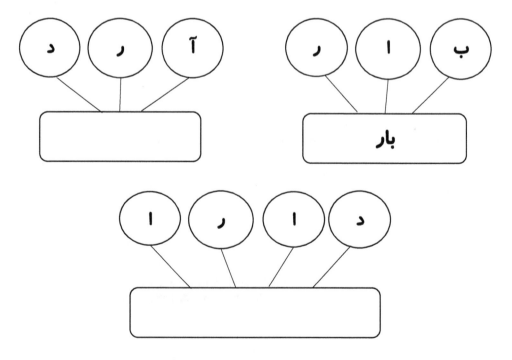

Exercise 16. Practice writing and pronouncing the following words in the space provided.

بابا بابا

دارا دارا

آب آب

داد داد

تاب تاب

آداب آداب

Exercise 17. Dictation: Listen to the audio file and write the words you hear in the following space. Listen as many times as necessary.

1. _____ 2. _____
3. _____ 4. _____
5. _____ 6. _____
7. _____ 8. _____
9. _____ 10. _____

Exercise 18. Identify the letters ا ب پ ت د ر by circling them in the following.

ن ک زار د ت م ی ل گ ی هزا د نا هب ار ت ی اپ.

برنامه‌ی زبان آموزی فارسی، بر اساس پژوهشهای علمی و آموزشی صاحبنظران و پژوهشگران شکل گرفته است.

5 Grammar

Word Stress

In Persian, all simple nouns and adjectives are stressed on the last syllable, as are nouns with plural suffixes, infinitives, and the negative prefix نَ /na/. (You will learn about the diacritics in the next lesson.)

Nouns	Adjectives	Nouns with Plural Suffix	Infinitives	The Negative Prefix نَ /na/
ā'-dāb'	zi-ba'	tāb-hā'	ā-ma-da'n	na'-ro
آ+داب=آداب	زی+با = زیبا	تاب + ها = تاب ها	آ+مَ+دَن = آمدن	نَ+رو = نَرو
(etiquette)	(beautiful)	(swings)	(to come)	(Don't go)

Formal and Spoken Registers in Persian

Register is used to indicate degrees of formality in language use in different types of situations and for different purposes, meaning that there is a close relationship between language and the context of the situation. For example, in a formal setting, a formal register would be appropriate, whereas in an informal setting a conversational and informal form is more suitable. It is important to note that the variation between the formal and informal in Persian is different than it is in English in both written and spoken forms.

In Persian, there are two registers, the formal register and the spoken register. Formal Persian is the language of books, magazines, newspapers, television news broadcasts, and formal speeches. Spoken Persian, on the other hand, is the language of daily conversation. A form of colloquial Tehrani Persian has become the general spoken standard of Modern Persian. However, local variations of the spoken colloquial Persian exist in the different regions and cities of Iran, for example, Isfahani, Shirazi, or Yazdi accents, to name a few. The spoken register that will be used in this book is the colloquial Tehrani Persian.

In order to become proficient in Persian, you need to learn both the formal and the spoken forms and know when to use the appropriate register, as there are differences in the pronunciation of the two registers. For example, the noun "bread" is /nān/ نان / in written Persian but /nun/ نون/ in the spoken form, or "I say," which is /migoyam/ می‌گویم/ in written Persian and /migam/ می‌گم/ in the spoken register.

In this lesson, you will be introduced to spoken Persian based on the conversational exchanges of native speakers in the listening and conversation section of the lesson. Each lesson in this book has a section on spoken Persian in the form of conversations in order for you to learn pronunciation variations. With listening and speaking practices and using the audios, you will learn the differences between the two registers over time

6 Listening and Conversation

Greetings and Replying to Greetings

The most common greeting in Persian is *salām*, which means "hi"/"hello" in English. As in English, people respond by repeating the greeting: *salām*. Response: *salām*. Following *salām*, it is often customary to inquire about the other interlocutor's (person taking part in a conversation) health by saying: *hāle shomā chetore?* (How are you?). The response is often a polite *khobam* (I am fine.) followed by thanking the inquirer and repeating the health-inquiry question: *shomā chetorid?* (How about you? How are you doing?). The first interlocutor responds with *khobam,* too.

Culture Note: As one enters a room, house, or place of work, it is customary to say *salām*. The response to this greeting is obligatory by those who are present in the room, house, or place of work. In addition, younger people are expected to greet older people first.

Introducing Yourself

In Persian, there are two different ways of introducing yourself. You may say *man (your name) hastam* (I am . . .), or *esme man (your name) e,* (*e* is the colloquial form of *ast* meaning *is*) which translates to (My name is . . .). It is important to note that for names that end in the long vowel *[ā]* such as *āryā*, the ending *s* rather than *e* is used, *esme man āryās* (My name is Arya). The common response to someone introducing themselves is *khoshvaqtam* (Nice to meet you).

Asking Others to Introduce Themselves

When you want to ask someone's name, you use the word اِسم /esm/, which you learned means "name," followed by the pronoun شما /shomā/ (the plural form of *you*), and the question word *chiye [chiye]* (the colloquial form of *chist* meaning "what is"). The question asking someone their name is, therefore, *esme shomā chiye?* (What is your name?).

🎧 Exercise 19.

A. Listen to the dialogue and practice each line several times. Be prepared to hold a similar conversation in class with your classmates.
B. Listen to the audio again and answer the questions:

1. What are the names of the two speakers? _____
2. Indicate which speaker makes each statement.

   a. *hāl-e shomā chetore?* _____
   b. *shomā chetorin?* _____
   c. *manam khubam, mamnun.* _____

Exercise 20. Class Activity.

Say hello to two classmates and ask them their names. Report their answers to the class.

🎧 Exercise 21.

A. Listen to the dialogue and practice each line several times. Be prepared to hold a similar conversation in class with your classmates.
B. Listen to the audio again and answer the questions:

1. to say Hello _____
2. to say Thank you _____

درس یک: سلام! چطوری؟ Hi! How Are You?

3. Indicate which speaker makes each statement.

a. esm-e shomā chiye? _____

b. khoshvaqtam _____

c. manam hamintor _____

🎧 **Exercise 22.**

A. Listen to the audio and practice each line several times. Be prepared to hold a similar conversation in class with your classmates.

B. Listen to the audio again and transcribe the dialogue using transliteration. Write your transcription in the space provided.

_____
_____

Exercise 23. Class Activity.

Go around the room and say hello to your classmates and teacher. Introduce yourself and make a list of your classmates' names.

🎧 *Listening and Conversation Vocabulary*

The following is a list of vocabulary related to the conversations. The list includes the spoken, as well as the written/formal, form of the vocabulary; their meaning; and their pronunciation using transliteration. The vocabulary terms are organized according to their appearance in the conversations.

Meaning	Transliteration	Written/Formal	Spoken/Colloquial
Hello/Hi	salām	سَلام	سَلام
How are you?	hāle shomā chetore?/ shomā chetor ast?	حالِ شُما چِطور است؟	حالِ شُما چِطوره؟
How are you?	shomā chetor hastid?	شُما چِطور هستید؟	شُما چِطورید؟
I/me	man	مَن	مَن
I'm fine.	khobam	خوبَم	خوبَم
Thank you	merci	مِرسی	مِرسی
Thank you	mamnun/mamnunam	مَمنونم	مَمنونم
I am	hastam	هَستم	هَستم
Your name	esme shomā	اِسمِ شُما	اِسمِ شُما
What is	chiye/chist	چیست	چیه

Meaning	Transliteration	Written/Formal	Spoken/Colloquial
Nice to meet you	khoshvaqtam	خوشوقتم	خوشوقتم
Nice to meet you	az didane shoma khoshvaqtam	از دیدن شما خوشوقتم	از دیدن شما خوشوقتم
Me too	manam hamintor/man ham hamintor	من هم همینطور	منم همینطور

Vocabulary Review Chart

English	Pronunciation	Persian
Water	āb	آب
Thriving	ābād	آباد
Etiquette	ādāb	آداب
Flour	ārd	آرد
Dad	bābā	بابا
Wind	bād	باد
Swing	tāb	تاب
He/she gave	dād	داد

Lesson 2

NICE TO MEET YOU! درس دو: آشنایی و معرفی

> **In this lesson you will learn:**
> - Letters
>
>   س ش
>   م ن
>   و ی
>
> - Long and Short Vowels
> - Grammar
>   - Syllable Structure
>   - Personal Pronouns
> - Listening and Conversation
>   - Morning Greetings
>   - Introducing Others
>   - Saying Goodbye

1 Letters

A. The Letter (sin) س

This letter is pronounced *[s]* as in the English word *sun* and has four different shapes. The letter س is a connecting letter with two or three *teeth (dandone)* depending on its position. In the freestanding and final positions, *sin* takes two *teeth* and in the initial and medial positions, it takes three. The final curve position of the letter descends below the line.

It should be noted that in the initial position, the letter connects to any letters following it, and in the medial position, it is a two-way connector, which means it connects both to letters that precede it as well as to letters that follow it. In the final position, however, it can only connect to letters that precede it.

Freestanding	Final	Medial	Initial
س	ـس	ـسـ	سـ

Exercise 1. Watch the video for how the shapes of the letter س are written. Trace the model letter, and then practice writing your own in the space provided and pronounce it as you write it.

B. The Letter (shin) ش

This letter is pronounced *[sh]* as in the word *she*. It is a connector, and its shapes are similar to س in all forms except that it has three dots placed above the letter. In the initial position, ش connects to following letters, but in the medial position, it can connect from both sides. In the final position, it can only connect to preceding letters.

Freestanding	Final	Medial	Initial
ش	ـش	ـشـ	شـ

Exercise 2. Watch the video for how the shapes of the letter ش are written. Trace the model letter, and then practice writing your own in the space provided and pronounce it as you write it.

Exercise 3. You will hear nine words, where each word contains either the letter س or ش. As you listen, circle the correct letter.

1. ش / س	2. ش / س	3. س / ش
4. س / ش	5. س / ش	6. ش / س
7. ش / س	8. س / ش	9. ش / س

Exercise 4. Join the letters in each set to form words, and then read the words. Remember to read from right to left.

1. س + ا + ر + ا   ←   ....

2. د + ا + س   ←   ....

3. آ + ش   ←   ....

4. ش + ا + د   ←   ....

5. پ + ا + س   ←   ....

6. س + ا + ر   ←   ....

7. آ + س + ا   ←   ....

C. The Letter (mim) م

This letter is a nasal labial sound, which resembles the English *[m]* as in the word *me*. It has four different shapes and connects depending on its position in a word. In other words, in the initial position it connects to following letters; in the medial position, it is a two-way connector that connects both to preceding letters as well as following letters. In the final position, it connects only to preceding letters. To write the letter م in the initial position, start on the line and make a small loop moving counterclockwise and then continue to make a short line. In the medial position, begin on the line moving up, then come back to make a small, loop and continue to make a short line. In the final position, make a small loop similar to the medial position, and then make a straight line going down below the line.

Freestanding	Final	Medial	Initial
م	م	م	م

Exercise 5. Watch the video for how the shapes of the letter م are written. Trace the model letter, then write your own letter in the space provided and pronounce it as you write it.

D. The Letter (nun) ن

This letter resembles the English sound *[n]* as in the word *no*. It is a connecting letter and has four different shapes. In the initial and medial forms, it resembles the letter ب but with the dot above the letter. In the final position, however, it descends below the line. In the initial position, ن connects to following letters, but in the medial position, it functions as a two-way connector and can connect from both sides. In the final position, it can only connect to preceding letters.

22 Nice to Meet You! درس دو: آشنایی و معرفی

Initial	Medial	Final	Freestanding
نـ	ـنـ	ـن	ن

Exercise 6. Watch the video for how the shapes of the letter ن are written. Trace the model letter, and then practice writing your own in the space provided and pronounce it as you write it.

Exercise 7. Listen to the audio, and circle the words that you hear.

3. ماست / ناست	2. باران / بارام	1. آرام / آران
6. نام / نان	5. آسمان / آسنان	4. تابان / تابام
9. آرمان / آرمام	8. ناب / ماب	7. نار / مار

Exercise 8. Read the following words. Remember to read from right to left.

3. شام	2. نام	1. آن
6. داشت	5. بادام	4. سارا
9. آرام	8. سامان	7. آسان
12. شاد	11. مامان	10. ماست
15. آبادان	14. باران	13. دانا

Exercise 9. Join the letters in each set to form words.

1. ش + ا + م ← ....
2. م + ا + ر ← ....
3. ا + س + ا + ن ← ....
4. م + ا + س + ت ← ....
5. ب + ا + ر + ا + ن ← ....
6. ا + ن + ا + ن + ا + س ← ....
7. د + ا + ن + ا ← ....
8. ا + ش + ن + ا ← ....
9. م + ا + م + ا + ن ← ....

Exercise 10. Circle the correct word for each picture.

باد
بار

آش نان	
شیر سیر	
آرد باران	
توت بادام	

Exercise 11. Practice writing the following words in the space provided, and pronounce them as you write them.

نام نام _____

شام شام _____

مار مار _____

شاد شاد _____

مامان مامان _____

آسمان آسمان _____

آناناس آناناس _____

🎧 **Exercise 12.** Dictation: Listen to the audio file and write the words you hear in the space below. Listen as many times as necessary.

1. _____
2. _____
3. _____
4. _____
5. _____
6. _____
7. _____
8. _____
9. _____
10. _____

E. The Letter (vāv) و

The letter *vāv* only has two forms, but it has more than one sound:

a. As a consonant, it resembles the English sound *[v]* as in the word *victory*. When و /vāv/ occurs in the initial position, it functions as a consonant and is pronounced *[v]* as in the word وام *[vām]* (loan). In an independent position, و is pronounced *[v]* as in the word گاو *[gāv]* (cow).

b. As a long vowel, و is pronounced *[u]* as in the English word *tooth*. It functions as a vowel, when in the medial and final positions. For example, it sounds *[u]* in the word دود *[dud]* (smoke). There are times when it may also occur as a long vowel in the beginning of a word, in which case it is preceded by *alef,* and is pronounced *[u]* as in the word او *[u]* (he/she).

c. *Vāv* may form a diphthong (a sound produced when two vowels are paired together in a sequence) pronounced *[ow]*, similar to the English word *blow*. An example is the Persian word نوروز *[nowruz]* (Iranian New Year).

d. Some Persian words that were pronounced with the long vowel *[u]* are pronounced with the short vowel */o/* in Modern Persian, for example, تو (you, singular) and دو (two).

e. When *vāv* is preceded by the letter خ *[khe]* and followed by a consonant, it is pronounced *[o]* in some words of Persian origin, as in the words, خود *[khod]* (self), خورشید *[khorshid]* (sun), and خوردن *[khordan]* (to eat). These words, too, were originally pronounced with the long vowel *[u]*, but they are pronounced as *[o]* in Modern Persian, although the spelling of the words has not changed.

f. In some words of Persian origin, *vāv is silent*, or as it is called *vāve ma'dule* (a *vāv* that is written but not pronounced). This silent و comes after the letter خ *[kh]*, as in the words خواب *[khāb]* (sleep) and خویش *[khish]* (self). (The silent و is discussed in more detail later in Lesson 6.)

Similar to the other one-way connectors, و has two forms, and it can only connect to preceding letters.

Connected from the right	Freestanding Position
ـو	و

Exercise 13. Watch the video for how the shapes of the letter و are written. Trace the model letter, and then practice writing your own in the space provided and pronounce it as you write it.

درس دو: آشنایی و معرفی Nice to Meet You! 27

🎧 **Exercise 14.** Listen to words containing the different sounds of و and repeat.

1. بو   2. او   3. بود

6. تو   7. دو   8. نو

11. آو   12. نانو   13. وام

Exercise 15. Join the letters in each set to form words.

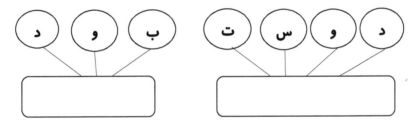

🎧 **Exercise 16.** Listen to the audio and circle the words that you hear.

1. دو / تو	2. مار / نار	3. سار / شار
4. آن / آم	5. دوست / پوست	6. ران / دان
7. را / دا	8. نان / مان	9. با / وا

F. The Letter (ye) ی

This letter, like the letter و, can represent more than one sound and can be regarded as either a consonant or a vowel.

a. When ی occurs in the initial position, it functions as a consonant and is pronounced similar to the English *[y]* as in the word *yet*.

b. As a long vowel, it is pronounced *[i]* as in the word *feel*. When ی is in the medial or final positions, as in the word سیب *[sib]* (apple) or سینی *[sini]* (tray), it is pronounced *[i]*. It may also occur as a long vowel in the beginning of a word. In such instances, ی is preceded by *alef* and is pronounced *[i]* as in the word این *[in]* (this).

درس دو: آشنایی و معرفی !Nice to Meet You

c. The letter ی may also function as a diphthong, in which case it is pronounced *[ey]* as in the English word *pay*. Examples of this sound in Persian are in words such as نِی *[ney]* (reed) and میدان *[meydān]* (field; square).

As a two-way connector, this letter has four forms. It resembles ت in the initial and medial forms except for the dots that are placed below the letter. However, the final and freestanding forms differ from the initial and medial forms, and they do not have dots. To write the final form, start on the line and continue making a curve below the line. For the freestanding ی, begin above the line and make a slight curve, then continue below the line and make another larger curve. This letter connects to the one on the left in the initial position, to both those on the left and right in the medial position, and only those to the right in the final position.

Freestanding	Final	Medial	Initial
ی	ی	ـیـ	یـ

Exercise 17. Watch the video for how the shapes of the letter ی are written. Trace the model letter, and then practice writing your own in the space provided and pronounce it as you write it.

Exercise 18. Listen to words containing the different pronunciations of ی and repeat.

1. یا   2. یاد   3. یاری   4. یاس   5. ایران
6. ایرانی   7. سیب   8. سیر   9. شیر   10. شیرینی

درس دو: آشنایی و معرفی !Nice to Meet You

Exercise 19. Join the letters in each set to form words.

1. ا + ب + ی ← ....
2. س + ی + ی ← ....
3. ا + ی + ر + ا + ن ← ....
4. ا + ی + ش + ا + ن ← ....
5. د + و + س + ت ← ....
6. ش + ا + د + ی ← ....
7. ر + ا + د + ی + و ← ....
8. ن + ی + م + ر + و ← ....
9. ی + ا + ر + ی ← ....

🎧 **Exercise 20.** Read the following words. Remember to read from right to left.

1. آیا	2. آبی	3. یاری	4. ایشان
5. شیمی	6. بیمار	7. بیدار	8. بیرون
9. سوت	10. توت	11. موش	12. ماشین
13. شادی	14. شیرینی	15. بینی	16. سینی
17. دوست	18. دوستی	19. ایران	20. ایرانی
21. تو	22. او	23. این	24. دوربین
25. یاس	26. یاد	27. یونان	28. رادیو

Exercise 21. Identify and write the letters of the following words in the space provided.

دوستی __ __ __ __ __ __
ایرانی __ __ __ __ __ __

30 Nice to Meet You! ‏درس دو: آشنایی و معرفی‎

Exercise 22. Join the letters in each set to form words.

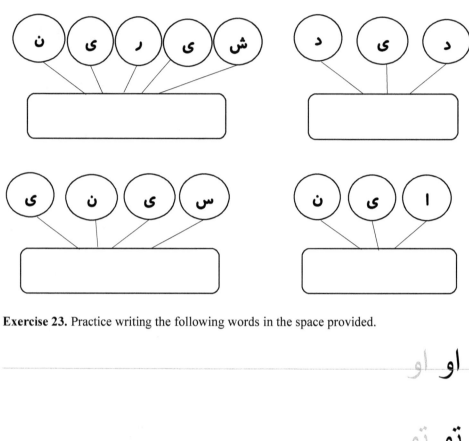

Exercise 23. Practice writing the following words in the space provided.

او او

تو تو

آیا آیا

ایشان ایشان

ایرانی ایرانی

بود بود

🎧 **Exercise 24. Dictation:** Listen to the words dictated to you and write them in the space provided. Listen as many times as needed.

1. _____
2. _____
3. _____
4. _____
5. _____
6. _____
7. _____
8. _____
9. _____
10. _____

Long and Short Vowels

In Lesson 1, you learned that Persian has three long vowels and three short vowels. The long vowel (ا *[ā]*) was covered in Lesson 1, and the other two long vowels (ای *[e]*) and (او *[u]*) were covered in the previous sections.

You also learned that short vowels are usually not written, and instead, diacritics may be used. Furthermore, vowels in the initial position are used with *alef*.

The three short vowels (ـَ *[a]*, / ـِ *[e]*, and ـُ *[o]*) correspond to their longer versions, respectively:

ـَ *[a]* with ا *[ā]*, ـِ *[e]* with ای *[e]* and ـُ *[o]* (with او *[u]*.

Here are the three short vowels:

Short Vowels as Diacritics	Sound	Short Vowels with *alef*	Sound
ـَ	[a] as in *at*	اَ	[a] as in *at*
ـِ	[e] as in *let*	اِ	[e] as in *let*
ـُ	[o] as in *home*	اُ	[o] as in *home*

📹 **Exercise 25.** Watch the video for how short vowels with *alef* are written. Then practice writing your own in the space provided and pronounce them as you write them.

اَ

اِ

اُ

32 Nice to Meet You! درس دو: آشنایی و معرفی

As mentioned earlier, short vowels are usually not written except during the elementary stages of learning the language and in cases in which it is difficult to distinguish homographs (words that have the same spelling but different pronunciation and meaning), for example, گَرم *[garm]* (hot) and گِرَم *[geram]* (gram). It is important to note that even in such cases, the use of diacritics (vowel signs) is optional as the reader is supposed to know the meaning from the context and from their own knowledge of the language.

In Lesson 1, you also learned that diacritics are placed above or below the letters to represent short vowel, for example, مَن *[man]* (I/me), مِداد *[medād]* (pencil), and تُند *[tond]* (fast). However, in the initial position, short vowels are written with *alef*, as in اَسب *[asb]* (horse), اِسم *[esm]* (name), and اُروپا *[orupā]* (Europe).

Exercise 26. Listen and repeat the following pair of words. The first word in each pair has a long vowel, and the second word has a short vowel.

3. بار / بَر	2. سار / سَر	1. تاب / تَب
6. مان / مَن	5. سام / سَم	4. تیم / تِم
9. مین / مِن	8. دین / دِن	7. سیم / سِم
12. سیر / سِر	11. دون / دُن	10. بور / بُر
15. مون / مُن	14. سور / سُر	13. بود / بُد

Exercise 27. Listen to the pronunciation of the following words and write their short vowel signs using diacritics (remember to use *alef* for the short vowel sounds in the initial position).

5. دریا	4. پدر	3. شما	2. ستاد	1. مادر
10. پسر	9. مید	8. دانش	7. نار	6. شب

Exercise 28. Complete the table below by adding the vowels (using letters and diacritics) to consonants given in the right-hand column, as in the example. Then read them aloud.

ی ی	و و	ِ	َ	ا ا	
بی	بو	بِ	بَ	با	بُ
					پ
					س
					ز
					ه
					ر

33 درس دو: آشنایی و معرفی !Nice to Meet You

Exercise 29. Join the letters and sounds in each set to form words (add *alef* as needed).

1. د + ܂ + ر   ←   ....
2. ت + ُ + ن + د   ←   ....
3. ِ + س + م   ←   ....
4. ܂ + س + ت   ←   ....
5. ܂ + ب + ر   ←   ....
6. ُ + س + ت + ا + د ←   ....
7. د + ܂ + ن + د + ا + ن ←   ....

Exercise 30. Form words as in the example and write them in the space provided.

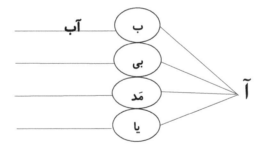

Exercise 31. Listen and identify whether each word you hear contains a long vowel, a short vowel, or both. Indicate your answer by checking the appropriate column.

	Long Vowel	Short Vowel
1		
2		
3		
4		
5		
6		
7		

Exercise 32. Practice reading each of the following words. Remember to read from right to left.

3. شَب	2. اَبر	1. مَرد
6. نَدارد	5. اَنار	4. مادَر
9. اَست	8. پسَر	7. اُمید
12. مَمنون	11. مرسی	10. اُستاد
15. دَست	14. دَندان	13. پدَر
18. دارَد	17. آداب	16. ادَب
21. نیستَم	20. اسپانیا	19. تابستان
24. پاسپورت	23. مترو	22. اُتوبوس
27. دانشمَند	26. رَوانشناس	25. پرَستار
30. می آیَم	29. می رَوَم	28. بسیار

Exercise 33. Identify and write the letters of the following words in the space provided. Make sure to include the diacritics.

پرَستار _ _ _ _ _ _ _

دانشمَند _ _ _ _ _ _ _

رَوانشناس _ _ _ _ _ _ _ _

Exercise 34. Practice writing the following words in the space provided.

اِسم اِسم

مَن مَن

شُما شُما

پسَر پسَر

مادَر مادَر

پِدَر پِدَر

اُستاد اُستاد

اَست اَست

🎧 **Exercise 35. Dictation:** Listen to the words dictated to you and write them in the space provided. Listen as many times as needed.

1. _____ 2. _____
3. _____ 4. _____
5. _____ 6. _____
7. _____ 8. _____
9. _____ 10. _____
11. _____ 12. _____

Exercise 36. Identify the letters س ش م ن و ی by circling them in the following:

دریای خزر بسیار زیبا و دیدنی می باشد
بوی یاس و محمدی می آید
می دانم فردا شب باران می آید
سالی که نکوست از بهارش پیداست

2 Grammar

Syllable Structure

In Persian, words consist of one or more syllables and the syllable structure is CV(C)(C), where "C" stands for consonant and "V" stands for vowel. There are three types of syllables, CV, CVC, and CVCC, which means that a syllable may have one, two, or three consonants but only one vowel (or diphthong). The syllable patterns with examples containing long and short vowels are illustrated in the following table.

Syllables	Examples	
CV	مو [mu] hair C + V (long vowel)	دو [do] two C + V (short vowel)
CVC	دور [dur] far C + V (long vowel) + C	دَر [dar] door C+ V (short vowel) + C
CVCC	پوست [pust] skin C + V (long vowel) + C + C	دَرد [dard] pain C +V (short vowel) + C+ C

All words, whether monosyllabic (consisting of one syllable) or polysyllabic (having more than one syllable) are formed according to the above configurations. Some points to consider in the Persian syllable structure:

1. There are no consonant clusters (when two consonants appear next to each other). Therefore, words that begin with two consonants are loanwords that are then Persian-ized, such as *[kelās] class*.
2. Syllables begin with a consonant sound. Even words that have a vowel in the initial position, include a glottal stop as the syllable onset, for example, /ʔabr/ cloud.
3. The second sound of each syllable is a vowel, as shown in the previous table.

Exercise 37. Complete the following chart by indicating the syllables and syllable patterns of the words given, as in the example.

Syllable Patterns	Syllables	Words
CV–CV	سی - نی	سینی
		بادام
		آسان
		می آیَم
		دانِشمَند
		رَوانشناس

🎧 Personal Pronouns

In Persian, personal pronouns can function both as subject and object pronouns. As subject pronouns, they denote the subject of the verb, and as object pronouns, they denote the object of the verb. For example: in the sentence, *man monā hastam* (I am Mona), مَن /man/ is the subject; however, in *ali man rā/marā did* (Ali saw me), مَن /man/ is the (direct) object, while Ali is the subject. The topic of direct objects is covered in future lessons.

The personal pronouns are listed in the following table.

	Person	Pronoun	Meaning	Pronunciation
Singular	First	مَن	I	*man*
	Second	تو	you	*to*
	Third	او	he/she/it	*u*
Plural	First	ما	we	*mā*
	Second	شُما	you	*shomā*
	Third	آنها/ایشان	they	*ānhā/ishān*

Important Notes about Personal Pronouns

- Since Persian is genderless, there is only one word to refer to English third-person singular pronouns—*he, she, it*—and that is او /u/.
- The second-person plural pronoun شُما /shomā/ is commonly used to refer to a second-person singular تو /to/ in formal situations in order to show respect, resembling the Spanish *usted* instead of *tu*.
- The third-person plural pronoun ایشان /ishān/ is often used to refer to a third-person singular او /u/ in formal spoken form for politeness.
- The pronoun, آنها /ānhā/, is more generally used to refer to third-person plural than ایشان because the latter is formal.

Exercise 38. Sort the personal pronouns into the boxes shown. Note that each pronoun should be written in more than one box.

آنها/ ایشان   شُما   ما   او   تو   مَن

First Person	Second Person	Third Person

Singular	Plural

Exercise 39. Use a Persian personal pronoun for the following:

To talk to your teacher _____
To talk to your friend(s) _____
To talk about yourself _____

3 Listening and Conversation

Morning Greetings

In Persian, the common greeting in the morning is *sobh bekheyr*, which translates to its English equivalent "Good morning." In this phrase, *sobh* means "morning," and *bekheyr* is "good." The proper response to *sobh bekheyr*, is either repeating the same phrase by the other person or saying *sobh-e shomā ham bekheyr*, which translates to "Good morning to you, too."

Introducing Others

In Lesson 1, you learned how to introduce yourself and inquire about someone's name. In this lesson, you will learn how to introduce someone else (i.e., family members, friends, colleagues, etc.). In Persian, in formal situations, you state the title of the person (Mr., Mrs., etc.) followed by their last name, for example:

آقای اَمینی / *āqā-ye amini* / (Mr. Amini)
خانُم اَمینی / *khanum-e amini* / (Mrs. Amini)

If you want to state the nature of the relationship when you introduce people as well (e.g., colleague, boss, etc.), you may add words like colleague or boss, before their title or after their name:

هَمکارِم ، خانُم اَمینی / *hamkāram, khānum-e amini* / (my colleague, Mrs. Amini)
خانُم اَمینی ، همکارم / *khānum-e amini, hamkāram* / (Mrs. Amini, my colleague)

In introducing family and relatives, on the other hand, you state the relationship first. Then, you follow with their name:

دُخترَم ، سارا / *dokhtaram, sārā* / (my daughter, Sara)
پسَرم ، اُمید / *pesaram, omid* / (my son, Omid)

In more formal situations, you state the family or relative's relationship followed by their titles (Mr., Mrs., etc.) and their last name:

مادَر بُزرگم ، خانُم اَمینی *mādar bozorgam, khānum amini* (my grandmother, Mrs. Amini)
For older individuals and for respect, titles of Mr. and Mrs. are used with first names:
پَری خانُم *pari khānum* (Mrs. Pari)
عَلی آقا *ali āqā* (Mr. Ali)

Saying Goodbye

At the time of leave-taking, *khodā hāfez* is a common parting expression that translates to "May God be with you" and is responded to by others with similar expressions *khodā hāfez* (colloquial: *khodāfez*) or *khodā negāhdār* (May God protect you).

🎧 **Exercise 40.**

A. Listen to the audio and practice each line several times. Be prepared to hold a similar conversation in class with your classmates.
B. Listen to the audio again and fill in the blanks.

- salām, sobh bekheyr
- ……………………….
- hale shomā? Khub …………………
- mamnonam, bad …………………… shomā …………………
- manam bad nistam.
- fe'lan ……………………..
- …………………………….

Exercise 41. Class Activity.

Go around the room. Say goodbye to your classmates and teacher.

🎧 **Exercise 42.**

A. Listen to the audio and practice each line several times. Be prepared to hold a similar conversation in class with your classmates.
B. Listen to the audio again and complete the table that follows.

	What did they say?
Nazy	
Maryam	
Leila	

Exercise 43. Class Activity.

Greet a classmate. Then introduce them to another classmate.

🎧 **Exercise 44.**

A. Listen to the audio and practice each line several times. Be prepared to hold a similar conversation in class with your classmates.
B. Listen to the audio again and transcribe the dialogue using transliteration. Write your transcription in the space provided.

درس دو: آشنایی و معرفی Nice to Meet You!

Exercise 45. Class Activity.

Introduce yourself to two of your classmates and ask them to introduce themselves.

🎧 Listening and Conversation Vocabulary

The following is a list of vocabulary related to the conversations. The list includes the spoken, as well as the written/formal, form of the vocabulary terms; their meaning; and their pronunciation using transliteration. The vocabulary terms are organized according to their appearance in the conversations.

Meaning	Transliteration	Written/Formal	Spoken/Colloquial
Good morning	sobh bekheyr	صُبح بخیر	صُبح بخیر
How are you?	khub hastin?/khub hastid?	خوب هَستید؟	خوب هَستین؟
(I'm) not bad	bad nistam	بَد نیستَم	بَد نیستَم
For now	fe'lan	فعلاً	فعلاً
Goodbye	khodāfez/khoda hāfez	خداحافظ	خدافظ
This	in	این	این
My friend	dustam	دوستم	دوستم
Professor	ostād	اُستاد	اُستاد
They are	hastan/hastand	هستند	هستن

Vocabulary Review Chart

English	Pronunciation	Persian
Easy	āsān	آسان
Pineapple	ānānās	آناناس
Cloud	abr	ابر
Is	ast	است
Pomegranate	anār	انار
Almond	bādām	بادام
Rain	bārān	باران
Father	pedar	پدَر

English	Pronunciation	Persian
Nurse	parastār	پَرَستار
Boy, son	pesar	پسَر
He/she has	dārad	دارَد
Ball	tup	توپ
Scientist	dāneshmand	دانشمَند
Psychologist	ravānshenās	رَوانشناس
Garlic	sir	سیر
Apple	sib	سیب
Happy	shād	شاد
Sweets	shirini	شیرینی
Mother	mādar	مادَر
Car	māshin	ماشین
Mom	māmān	مامان
Pencil	medād	مِداد
Mouse	mush	موش
I come	miāyam	می آیَم
I go	miravam	می رَوَم

Lesson 3

WHAT'S THIS?

درس سه: این چیست؟

In this lesson you will learn:

- Letters

  خ ح ج چ

- Persian Numbers 0–10 (۰–۱۰)
- Letters

  ز ژ
  ه

- Grammar

  - Demonstrative Pronouns and Adjectives
  - Present Tense of the Verb "To Be"
  - Word Order

- Listening and Conversation

  - What Is This called?

---

1 Letters

A. The Letter (jim) ج

The letter *jim* is pronounced *[j]*, similar to the English letter *j* in *jump*. The top stroke is written first above the line followed by a curve-like shape below the line. This letter has four different forms and in the initial and medial positions, the letter loses its tail-like curve. All forms have one dot, where it is placed below the line in the final and medial positions and inside the curve in the final and freestanding positions. The letter *jim* connects to a following

43   درس سه: این چیست؟ What's This?

letter in the initial position, and in the medial position, it can connect from both sides. In the final position, *jim* can only connect to a preceding letter.

Freestanding	Final	Medial	Initial
ج	ج	ـجـ	جـ

📹 **Exercise 1.** Watch the video for how the shapes of the letter ج are written. Trace the model letter, and then write your own letter in the space provided and pronounce it as you write it.

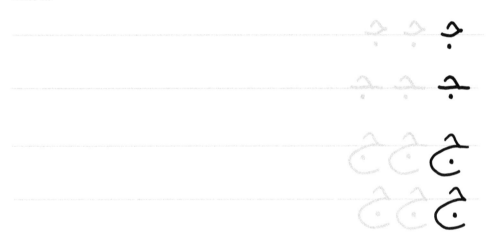

B. The Letter (che) چ

The letter *che* is pronounced similar to the English letter *ch* in *church*. It is written similarly to the letter ج but has three dots instead of one. There are four different forms of this letter, and its connectivity is the same as the letter ج.

Freestanding	Final	Medial	Initial
چ	چ	ـچـ	چـ

📹 **Exercise 2.** Watch the video for how the shapes of the letter چ are written. Trace the model letter, and then write your own letter in the space provided and pronounce it as you write it.

44 What's This? درس سه: این چیست؟

C. The Letter (ḥe) ح

The pronunciation of the letter ḥe is similar to the English letter *h* in *house*. It is written similarly to the letters ج and چ but with no dots. There are four different forms of this letter, and its connectivity is the same as the letters ج and چ.

Freestanding	Final	Medial	Initial
ح	ـح	ـحـ	حـ

📹 **Exercise 3**. Watch the video for how the shapes of the letter ح are written. Trace the model letter, and then write your own letter in the space provided and pronounce it as you write it.

D. The Letter (khe) خ

The Persian letter *khe* is similar to the German *ch* in the word *Bach*. *ch* was part of the consonant inventory of Old English and can still be found in some dialects of English, most notably in Scottish English *loch*. This voiceless consonant is articulated with the back part of the tongue against the soft palate. The Persian *khe* is written similarly to the letters ج, چ and ح, but unlike ح and چ, it has one dot placed above the line. There are four different forms of this letter, and its connectivity is the same as the letters چ, ج, and ح.

Freestanding	Final	Medial	Initial
خ	ـخ	ـخـ	خـ

Exercise 4. Watch the video for how the shapes of the letter خ are written. Trace the model letter, and then write your own letter in the space provided and pronounce it as you write it.

Exercise 5. You will hear 12 words, where each word contains either ح, چ, ج, or خ. As you listen to each word, determine which letter you hear and circle it.

1. خ / چ / ج / ح
2. ح / خ / ج / چ
3. چ / ح / ج / خ
4. چ / ج / خ / ح
5. ح / ج / خ / چ
6. خ / ح / چ / ج
7. خ / ج / ح / چ
8. خ / چ / ج / ح
9. چ / ح / خ / ج
10. ح / خ / چ / ج
11. ح / چ / خ / ج
12. ج / خ / ح / چ

درس سه: این چیست؟

Exercise 6. Join the letters in each set to form words, and then read the words. Remember to read from right to left.

1. چ + َ- + ن + د ← ....
2. ت + َ- + خ + ت ← ....
3. خ + َ- + ب + َ- + ر ← ....
4. ج + َ- + و + ا + ن ← ....
5. چ + ِ- + ش + م ← ....
6. ج + َ- + ن + پ ← ....
7. چ + ی + س + ت ← ....
8. د + ُ- + خ + ت + َ- + ر ← ....
9. ن + ا + ر + ِ- + ن + ج + ی ← ....
10. ح + ِ- + س + ا + د + ا + ر ← ....

Exercise 7. Read the following words. Remember to read from right to left.

3. خوب	2. آنجا	1. اینجا
21. چین	20. جَشن	19. خوش
9. دانِشجو	8. جَوان	7. جَواب
12. خورشید	11. دُختَر	10. درَخت
15. چیست	14. چِرا	13. چای
18. چَند	17. نارِنجی	16. جوراب

درس سه: این چیست؟ What's This?

🎧 **Exercise 8.** You will hear pairs of letters. Write the letters you hear in the space provided.

_____ _____ .1   _____ _____ .2   _____ _____ .3
_____ _____ .4   _____ _____ .5   _____ _____ .6
_____ _____ .7   _____ _____ . 8   _____ _____ . 9

Exercise 9. Add the initial form of the letter ج to each set of letters, and then write the word in the blank space provided.

.1 □ +ا+ی= □   .3 □ +ون = □

.2 □ +ِ-+را = □   .4 □ +-َ+ذ= □

Exercise 10. Write the letters of the following words in the space provided.

چینی _ _ _ _
تاریخ _ _ _ _ _
اینجا _ _ _ _ _

Exercise 11. Practice writing the following words in the space provided.

چِرا

پَنج

دُختَر

جَوان

دِانشجو

نارِنجی

چیست

درس سه: این چیست؟ What's This?

🎧 **Persian Numbers 0 – 10**

Numbers in Persian are written from left to right as in English. Numbers 0 to 10 are

Numerals	In Letters	Pronunciation	In English
۰	صِفر	ṣefr	0
۱	یِک	yek	1
۲	دو	do	2
۳	سه	se	3
۴	چَهار	chahār	4
۵	پَنج	panj	5
۶	شِش	shesh	6
۷	هَفت	haft	7
۸	هَشت	hasht	8
۹	نُه	noh	9
۱۰	دَه	dah	10

In spoken Persian, numbers 4 and 6 are pronounced as follows:

1. *Chahār* is pronounced *chāhār* or *chār* (with the drop of the *[h]*).
2. *Shesh* is pronounced *shish*.

🎬 **Exercise 12.** Watch the video for how the numbers are written. Then write your own in the space provided, and pronounce them aloud as you write them.

    ۱۰

🎧 **Exercise 13.** Listen to the audio and circle the number you hear in each set.

1. ۶, ۵, ۴
2. ۷, ۸, ۹
3. ۳, ۲, ۵
4. ۱, ۳, ۲
5. ۴, ۹, ۶
6. ۱۰, ۸, ۱
7. ۸, ۶, ۷
8. ۵, ۴, ۳

Exercise 14. Answer the following questions using Persian numbers.

How many siblings do you have? _____
What is your favorite number? _____

Exercise 15. Class Activity
With a partner, take turns counting from zero to ten in intervals of 2 and 3.

🎧 **Exercise 16. Dictation:** Listen to the words dictated to you and write them in the space that follows.

۲. _____   ۱. _____
۴. _____   ۳. _____
۶. _____   ۵. _____
۸. _____   ۷. _____
۱۰. _____   ۹. _____
۱۲. _____ ۱۱. _____

روز بِخیر

E. The Letter (ze) ز

There are four letters in Persian that have the *[z]* sound, and the letter *(ze)* is the first of the four you will be learning. Its pronunciation is similar to the English sound *[z]* in zoo. Ze has the same shape as ر with the addition of one dot above, and its connectivity is the same, as well. In other words, it does not connect to a following letter.

Connected from the right	Freestanding Position
ـز	ز

🎥 **Exercise 17.** Watch the video for how the shapes of the letter ز are written. Trace the model letter, and then write your own letter in the space provided and pronounce it as you write it.

درس سه: این چیست؟ What's This?

F. The Letter (zhe) ژ

This letter is similar to the English sound *[ʒ]* in *pleasure* and *leisure*. It is written similarly to ر and ز, but it takes three dots above. Its connectivity is the same as ر and ز.

Connected from the right	Freestanding Position
ـژ	ژ

Exercise 18. Watch the video for how the shapes of the letter ژ are written. Trace the model letter, and then write your own letter in the space provided and pronounce it as you write it.

Exercise 19. You will hear nine words containing either ز or ژ. As you listen to each word, determine whether it has ز or ژ and then circle it.

Exercise 20. Join the letters in each set to form words, then read the words. Remember to read from right to left.

۱. ز + ـَ + ن
۲. ژ + ی + ب + ا
۳. م + ی + ژ
۴. ژ + ـَ + ر + د
۵. ز + ـَ + ب + ا + ن
۶. ا + ش + پ + ـَ + ز
۷. د + ی + ر + و + ز

....
....
....
....
....
....
....

51 درس سه: این چیست؟ What's This?

۸. ب + ا + ز + ا + ر ....
۹. پ + ا + س + ا + ژ ....
۱۰. ژ + ا + پ + ـُ + ن ....

Exercise 21. Write the letters and diacritics of the words in the space provided

۱. میز ــ ــ ــ
۲. زَنبور ــ ــ ــ ــ ــ
۳. نوروز ــ ــ ــ ــ ــ

🎧 **Exercise 22.** Listen to the pronunciation of the words and write their short vowel signs. Remember to use *alef* for the short vowel sounds in the initial position.

مروز	سبز	زمین	زبان	زیتون
آشپز	بیژن	ژاپنی	پژمان	زمستان

Exercise 23. Write six words that contain one of the letters ج چ ح خ ر ز in the space provided.

۱. _____   ۲. _____   ۳. _____
۴. _____   ۵. _____   ۶. _____

🎧 **Exercise 24.** For each number below, you will hear three words. Two of the words will be the same. Write **a** if you hear the first one as different, **b** if the second, or **c** if you hear the third one as different.

۱. _____   ۲. _____   ۳. _____
۴. _____   ۵. _____   ۶. _____

Exercise 25. Read the following words. Remember to read from right to left.

۳. دیروز	۲. امروز	۱. روز
۶. شَب بخیر	۵. رَوز بخیر	۴. نوروز
۹. زَن	۸. زَبان	۷. زَمان
۱۲. بیژن	۱۱. ژاپُن	۱۰. آژانس
۱۵. زرد	۱۴. سبزی	۱۳. سَبز
۱۸. زیاد	۱۷. زیبا	۱۶. زِمستان
۲۱. شیراز	۲۰. داروساز	۱۹. سَرباز

درس سه: این چیست؟ What's This?

Exercise 26. Listen to the audio, and circle the words that you hear.

| ۳. اِنرژی / اِنرجی | ۲. ژاپُن / جاپُن | ۱. تاج / تاژ |
| ۶. بیژَن / بیجَن | ۵. موژان / موجان | ۴. آجانس / آژانس |

Exercise 27. Practice writing the following words in the space provided.

زَن زَن

زَبان زَبان

زیبا زیبا

اِمروز اِمروز

دیروز دیروز

ژاپن ژاپن

شیراز شیراز

Exercise 28. Complete the following words by filling out the missing letter indicated by the space between the letters. The missing letters are د - ر - ز - ژ. Add diacritics as needed.

۱. نا. . .نجی   ۲. . . .رَخت   ۳. . . .نبور   ۴. اِم. . .وز   ۵. آ. . .انس
۶. سَ. . .ی   ۷. زَ. . .د   ۸. . . .اِنش   ۹. میـ. . .   ۱۰. سَربا. . .

درس سه: این چیست؟ What's This?

🎧 **Exercise 29. Dictation:** Listen to the words dictated to you and write them in the space that follows.

٢. _____	١. _____
۴. _____	٣. _____
۶. _____	۵. _____
٨. _____	٧. _____
١٠. _____	٩. _____
١٢. _____	١١. _____

G. The Letter (he) ه

The letter ه /he/ is often pronounced the same as ح in Persian, as in حامِد. Native speakers may distinguish between the two by referring to ح as *he-ye jimi*, which translates to *the ح that resembles ج* because it has the same shape. And referring to ه as *he-ye do cheshh*, meaning *the /he/ of two eyes*, because in its initial position, this letter resembles *having two eyes*: ه. That said, there are four different forms of this letter, with each one written differently, as shown in the following table.

Freestanding	Final	Medial	Initial
ه	ه	ـهـ	هـ

This letter connects to a following letter in the initial position, but in the medial position, it can connect from both sides. In the final position, it can only connect to a preceding letter. It is important to note that similar to و and ی, this letter functions both as a consonant and a vowel.

ه has the sound *[h]* and functions as a consonant when it occurs in the initial, medial, and freestanding positions:

māh (moon)   chahār (four)   hasht (eight)

It functions as a vowel and represents the sound *[e]* when it occurs in the final position. If ه is preceded by a consonant in the freestanding position, it sounds *[e]* as well:

54 What's This? درس سه: این چیست؟

خانه   تازه

tāze (fresh)   *khane* (house)

Exercise 30. Watch the video for how the shapes of the letter ه are written. Trace the model letter, and then write your own letter in the space provided and pronounce it as you write it.

Exercise 31. Listen to words containing the different sounds of ه and repeat.

1. ماهی   2. بَهار   3. خانه   4. شَهر   5. ماه

6. هَمه   7. آهو   8. آره   9. چیه   10. خَسته

Exercise 32. Read the following words. Remember to read from right to left.

۱. ماه	۲. بَهار	۳. هَوا
۴. مُهَندِس	۵. مِهربان	۶. هَست
۷. هُنَر	۸. هُنَرمَند	۹. نویسَنده
۱۰. مِهمان	۱۱. هَم	۱۲. هَستَم
۱۳. آره	۱۴. شَهر	۱۵. تِهران
۱۶. هِند	۱۷. هَواپیما	۱۸. پیاده

درس سه: این چیست؟ What's This?

Exercise 33. Join the letters in each set to form words.

1. ن +ُ- + ه ← ....
2. ه +َ- + + م + ه ← ....
3. ه +َ- + و + ا ← ....
4. آ + ن + ه + ا ← ....
5. خ + ا + ن + ه ← ....
6. ش +َ- + ه + ر ← ....
7. ب +َ- + ه + ا + ر ← ....
8. ی + ا +َ- + ز + د +َ- + ه ← ....
9. م +َ-+ د +َ- + ر +ِ- + س + ه ← ....
10. ه +َ- + س + ت + ی + م ← ....

Exercise 34. Read the following words. Remember to read from right to left.

۳. چه خوب	۲. خانواده	۱. خانه
۶. هَستیم	۵. همیشه	۴. همه
۹. هَستَند	۸. دوچَرخه	۷. اینها
۱۲. نیستیم	۱۱. خَسته	۱۰. نَه
۱۵. خوبه	۱۴. چیه	۱۳. مَدرِسه

درس سه: این چیست؟ What's This? 56

Exercise 35. Add the appropriate form of ه ﻪ ﻬ ﺔ to complete each word, and then read them aloud.

۱. ما — ۲. میو — ۳. نام — ۴. خاز —
۵. ــُـست ۶. ــُـوا ۷. بــار ۸. چیـ —

Exercise 36. Practice writing the following words in the space provided.

آنها

بَهار بَهار

ماه ماه

تِهران تِهران

خانواده خانواده

مِهربان مِهربان

هَستَند هَستَند

درس سه: این چیست؟ What's This?

🎧 **Exercise 37. Dictation:** Listen to the words dictated to you and write them in the space provided.

1. _____
2. _____
3. _____
4. _____
5. _____
6. _____
7. _____
8. _____
9. _____
10. _____
11. _____
12. _____

Exercise 38. Identify the letters ج چ ح خ ز ژ ه by circling them in the following:

جانا سخن از زبان ما می گویی

خلیج فارس در جنوب ایران بسیار زیباست

گنجشک و جوجه هر روز جیک جیک می کنن

دیروز در راه یک ماشین پژو با ماشین ژیان

ژیلا و مُژگان برخورد کرد. راننده ی پژو به اسم بیژن به شدت آسیب

دید و با آمبولانس به اورژانس رفت.

دیروز در راه یک ماشین پژو با ماشین ژیان ژیلا و مُژگان برخورد کرد.

راننده ی پژو به اسم بیژن به شدت آسیب دید و با آمبولانس به اورژانس

رفت.

درس سه: این چیست؟

Exercise 39. Class Activity

Dictation: Work with a partner, where one of you will be Student 1 and the other Student 2 giving each other a dictation. Student 1 will be reading List A, and Student 2 will be reading List B.

Step 1: Student 1 covers up List B.
Step 2: Student 1 spells aloud the words from List A for Student 2 to write down.
Step 3: Student 2 writes down the words.
Step 4: Student 2 spells aloud the words from List B as Student 1 writes them down.

List A	List B
چای	چِرا
چیه	دُختَر
روز بِخیر	دانِشجو
خانواده	زَبان
خَسته	هَست
هَستید	آنها
بَهار	نوروز
اینها	مِهرَبان
تِهران	خوشمَزه
هَستیم	هَستَند

2 Grammar

Demonstrative Pronouns and Adjectives

The demonstratives این and آن are used to point something out. این points to something that is close, and آن points to a something that is far. The demonstrative pronouns این and آن replace nouns, and like nouns, they can be made into plural: اینها / این ها /inha/ (these) and آنها /آن ها /anha/ (those). (ها /ha/ is a plural marker that is discussed in later lessons.)

Exercise 40. Read the following:

این چیست؟ این آنار است.	این چیه؟ این آناره.
آن چیست؟ آن آناناس است.	اون چیه؟ اون آناناسه.

*In spoken Persian, است + چی (چیست) becomes چیه and اَست becomes ه / ه, and it is pronounced /e/.

When این and آن are modified by a noun, they are considered demonstrative adjectives:

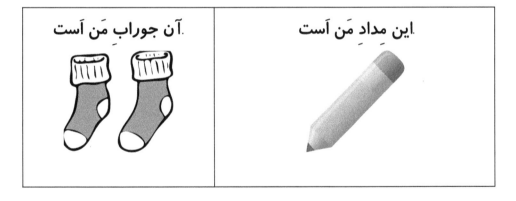

آن جورابِ مَن است.	این مِدادِ مَن است.

درس سه: این چیست؟ What's This?

Exercise 41. Fill in the blanks using a demonstrative pronoun: این ، آن ، اینها ، آنها

۱. _____ سیب اَست.	
۲. _____ موز هَستَند.	
۳. _____ آهو هَستَند.	
۴. _____ اَسب اَست.	
۵. _____ شیر اَست.	
۶. _____ ماهی اَست.	

Present Tense of the Verb "To Be" بودَن

The present tense of the verb "to be," بودَن, has two forms, a long form and a short form. The long forms are discussed in this lesson and the short forms in the next lesson.

In the formation of the present tense, the present stem of the infinitive بودَن is used. The present stem هَست is conjugated in the following table. It should be noted that the use of the present stem in forming the present tense applies to all other Persian verbs as well.

Long Form of the Verb "To Be" بودَن

We are	هَستیم /hastim/	I am	هَستَم /hastam/
You are (pl.)	هَستید /hastid/	You are	هَستی /hasti/
They are	هَستَند /hastand/	S/he/it is	*هَست/اَست /hast – ast/

* The third person singular هَست also has the meaning "There is." For example, آب هَست؟/ āb hast/ means, "Is there water?" or "Is there water here?" The respond to this question is, بله ، آب هَست /bale āb hast/, which means "Yes, there is water." However, the sentence, آب سَرد است /āb sard ast/ means "The water is cold." Therefore, unlike the former question, this statement is no longer about the presence of water but, rather, the property of water.

In the example, آب در پارچ هَست؟ /āb dar parch hast/, meaning "Is there water in the jar?" the question seeks clarification of whether there is water in the jar; hence, the presence of water. But in آب در پارچ است /āb dar parch ast/, meaning "Water is in the jar," there is reference to where the water is, which is, in the jar. So the use of است is not a question of the presence or absence of water but of where the water is.

Exercise 42. Read the following:

این جان آست   مَن سارا هَستَم
او دانِشجو است   مَن دانِشجو هَستَم
جان ایرانی نیست   مَن ایرانی هَستَم

The Negation. The negative form of هَست/است is نیست /nist/ (is not). By conjugating نیست, the negative forms of "to be" are made as shown in the table that follows.

Negative Form of the Verb "To Be"

We are not	نیستیم /nistim/	I am not	نیستَم /nistam/
You are not (pl.)	نیستید /nistid/	You are not	نیستی /nisti/
They are not	نیستَند /nistand/	S/he/ is not	نیست /nist/

Spoken Form of "To Be"

In spoken Persian, اَست is changed to ه, pronounced /-e/ and connected to a preceding consonant:

درس سه: این چیست؟ What's This?

خوب اَست ← خوبه

After a long vowel, *alef* is dropped from اَست as follows:

دانِشجو اَست ← دانِشجوست

The verb ending for second- and third-person plural changes as follows:

هَستید ← هَستین

هَستَند ← هَستَن

Exercise 43. Complete each sentence using a pronoun or the correct form of the verb "to be."

۱. مَن دانشجو _____ .
۲. _____ خوب هستی؟
۳. شما ایرانی _____ ؟
۴. آنها اُستاد _____ .
۵. _____ ژاپُنی است.
۶. آن مادَر _____ . (Negative)
۷. _____ چینی هستید؟
۸. آنها ایرانی _____ (Negative).
۹. این پدَر _____ .
۱۰. _____ شاد اَست.

Word Order

In Persian, the normal word order is subject (S)–object (O)–verb (V) → (SOV). For example, in the sentence اُمید خوب اَست /omid khub ast/ (Omid is fine), the subject is اُمید /omid/ (Omid), and the predicate is خوب اَست /khub ast/ (is fine). The predicate is the part of the sentence that includes the verb, object, and/or complement but not the subject. It is important to note that the verb almost always comes at the end of a sentence, as shown in the earlier sentence. In addition, in Persian, only verb phrases can act as predicates. (A verb phrase is the part of a sentence that contains a verb and its dependents, a direct or indirect object.)

In another example, سارا اَنار دارَد /sārā anār dārad/ (Sara has a pomegranate), the subject is سارا (Sara), the object is اَنار /anār/ (pomegranate), and the verb is دارَد /dārad/ (has). The verb دارَد is discussed in detail in Lesson 6.

🎧 **Exercise 44. Dictation:** Listen to the sentences and write them in the space provided.

۱. _____
۲. _____
۳. _____

۴. _____
۵. _____
۶. _____
۷. _____
۸. _____

3 Listening and Conversation

What Is This Called?

Listen to and practice the conversations in this section. Learn how to form a question asking what something is called and how to respond to the question.

🎧 **Exercise 45**.
A. Listen to the audio and practice each line several times. Be prepared to hold a similar conversation in class with your classmates.
B. Listen to the audio again and complete the name of the items you hear.

1. م _____   2. ن _____   3. م _____

4. س _____   5. م _____   6. س _____

7. ش _____   8. د _____   9. پ _____

Exercise 46. Class Activity.

Draw pictures of three fruits from the lesson's vocabulary and put them on a desk. Ask your partner to name the items and spell their name. Use, " این چیه؟ ." Reverse roles, where your partner draws pictures of three animals and you say what they are and spell their name using the previous question.

🎧 **Exercise 47**.
A. Listen to the audio and practice each line several times. Be prepared to hold a similar conversation in class with your classmates.
B. Listen to the audio again and fill in the blanks.

- سلام ، خانم بزرگ نیا. حالتون چطوره؟
- سلام. _____ جان. خوبم. مرسی. شما چطورین؟
- خیلی خوبم. اینا چی _____ ؟
- این _____ ، این _____ ، این _____ ، این _____ ، اینم _____ .

- من _____ دوست دارم. شما چطور؟
- من آنار دوست دارم ، _____ و _____ و شیر و _____ دوست دارم.
- چه خوب!

خداحافظ

🎧 Listening and Conversation Vocabulary

The following is a list of vocabulary terms related to the conversations. The list includes the spoken, as well as the written/formal, form of the vocabulary; their meaning; and pronunciation using transliteration. The vocabulary terms are organized according to their appearance in the conversations.

Meaning	Transliteration	Written/Formal	Spoken/Colloquial
Ready	hāzer	حاضِر	حاضِر
Yes	āreh/bale	بَله	آره
My flight	pārvāzam	پَروازَم	پَروازَم
It is 8 o'clock	sā'at hashte	ساعَت هَشت اَست	ساعَت هَشته
All	hame	هَمه	هَمه
Things	chizhā	چیزها	چیزها
Picked up	bardāshti	بَرداشتی	بَرداشتی
My whistle	sutam	سوتَم	سوتَم
Ticket	bilit/belit	بلیت	بیلیت
Where is	kojāst	کُجا است	کُجاست
Have a good time	khosh begzare	خوش بِگُذَرد	خوش بِگذَره
So	pas	پَس	پَس
Camera	durbin	دوربین	دوربین
I like	dust dāram	دوست دارَم	دوست دارَم
How nice	che khub	چه خوب	چه خوب
Wow how happy I am	vāy cheqad/cheqadr khoshhālam	وای چِقَدر خوشحالَم	وای چِقَد خوشحالَم

Vocabulary Review Chart

English	Pronunciation	Persian
Spring	bahār	بَهار
Sock	jurāb	جوراب
Tea	chāy	چای
Eye	cheshm	چشم
Why	cherā	چرا
Several, how many	chand	چند
Family	khānevāde	خانواده
House, home	khāne	خانه
Tired	khaste	خَسته
Delicious	khoshmaze	خوشمَزه
College student	dāneshju	دانشجو
Girl, daughter	dokhtar	دُختَر
Bicycle	docharkhe	دوچَرخه
Good day	ruz bekheyr	روز بخیر
Language, tongue	zābān	زَبان
Winter	zemestān	زمستان
Woman, wife	zan	زن
Japanese	zhāponi	ژاپُنی
Soldier	sārbāz	سرباز
City	shahr	شَهر
Moon, month	māh	ماه
Guest	mehmān	مهمان
Engineer	mohandes	مهندس
Fruit	mive	میوه
Writer	nevisande	نویسَنده
Always	hamishe	همیشه
Art	honar	هُنَر
Artist	honarmand	هُنَرمَند
Airplane	hāvāpeymā	هواپیما

Lesson 4

WHAT DO YOU DO?

درس چهار: شغل شما چیست؟

> **In this lesson you will learn:**
>
> - Letters
>
>   ص   ض
>   - Persian Numbers 11–20 (۱۱ – ۲۰)
> - Letters
>
>   ط   ظ
>   ع   غ
>   ل
> - Grammar
>   - Short Form of the Verb "To Be"
>   - Ezafe
> - Listening and Conversation
>   - Asking Someone What Job They Do
>   - Talking About What Job You Do

1 Letters

A. The Letter (ṣād) ص

The voiceless consonant *ṣād* is a fricative (a sound made by forcing air out of your mouth through a narrow opening) that has the same sound as س. The top part of the letter has an oval shape followed by a round curve below the line, all written in one stroke. *Ṣād* shares a similar shape in the freestanding and final positions. It connects to a following letter in the initial position, but in the medial position, it can connect from both sides. In the final position, it can only connect to a preceding letter. There are four different forms of this letter as shown in the following table.

Freestanding	Final	Medial	Initial
ص	ـص	ـصـ	صـ

Exercise 1. Watch the video for how the shapes of the letter ص are written. Trace the model letter, and then practice writing your own in the space provided and pronounce it aloud.

B. The Letter (żād) ض

The letter żād, a voiced fricative consonant, has the same sound as ز and a similar shape to ص except that it has one dot above. There are four different forms of this letter, and its connectivity is the same as ص, as shown in the table that follows.

Freestanding	Final	Medial	Initial
ض	ـض	ـضـ	ضـ

Exercise 2. Watch the video for how the shapes of the letter ض are written. Trace the model letter, and then practice writing your own in the space provided and pronounce it aloud.

68 What Do You Do? درس چهار: شغل شما چیست؟

🎧 **Exercise 3.** Listen to the following words and repeat.

۴. صُحبَت	۳. مَخصوص	۲. صابون	۱. صُبح
۸. مَریض	۷. حاضِر	۶. ریاضی	۵. راضی

Exercise 4. Join the letters in each set to form words.

۱. ص + ‑ + د + ا ← ....

۲. ص + ‑ُ + ب + ح ← ....

۳. ر + ‑ + ض + ا ← ....

۴. ص + ا + ب + و + ن ← ....

۵. ص + ‑ُ + ح + ب + ‑َ + ت ← ....

۶. م + ‑ + ص + ر ← ....

۷. ص + و + ر + ‑َ + ت + ی ← ....

۸. ر + ی + ا + ض + ی ← ....

۹. ص + ‑ُ + ب + ح + ا + ن + ه ← ....

۱۱. م + ‑َ + ر + ی + ض ← ....

۱۲. ح + ا + ض + ‑ + ر ← ....

درس چهار: شغل شما چیست؟ What Do You Do?

Exercise 5. Read the following words. Remember to read from right to left.

1. صَد	2. صُبح	3. صُبح بخیر
4. صدا	5. صَبا	6. صابون
7. مَریض	8. حاضر	9. ریاضی
10. صُحبَت	11. صورَت	12. صورَتی
13. خاص	14. مَخصوص	15. مِصر

Exercise 6. Find examples of the letters in the right column and circle them.

Letter	List of Letters									
ص	س	ض	ی	ص	ش	ی	ض	س	ح	س
ج	ح	چ	ب	ج	خ	چ	ج	ن	ی	خ	چ
د	ر	ز	ژ	د	م	و	ز	د	ص	و	ر
ض	ج	ذ	ض	ص	خ	ش	ض	خ	ج	ز	خ

Exercise 7. Practice writing the following words in the space provided.

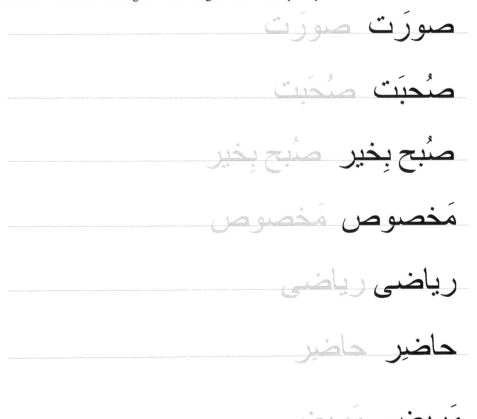

Exercise 8. Make words. The text in the circle added to the beginning of the content of each of the four boxes makes a word. Write the words you make in the space provided, as in the example.

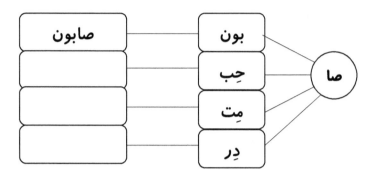

🎧 **Persian Numbers 11–20**

In Lesson 3, you learned that Persian numbers are written from left to right. You also learned numbers zero through 10. In this lesson, you will learn numbers 11 through 20.

Numerals	In Letters	Pronunciation	In English
۱۱	یازدَه	yāzdah	11
۱۲	دوازدَه	davāzdah	12
۱۳	سیزدَه	sizdah	13
۱۴	چهاردَه	chahārdah	14
۱۵	پانزدَه	pānzdah	15
۱۶	شانزدَه	shānzdah	16
۱۷	هفدَه	hefdah	17
۱۸	هجدَه	hejdah	18
۱۹	نوزدَه	nozdah	19
۲۰	بیست	bist	20

In colloquial Persian numbers 14 through 18 are pronounced, as follows:

1. *chahārdah* is pronounced *chāhārdah* or *chārdah* (with the drop of the *[h]*).
2. *pānzdah* is pronounced *punzdah*.
3. *shānzdah* is pronounced *shunzdah*.
4. *hefdah* is pronounced *hevdah*.
5. *hejdah* is pronounced *hezhdah*.

Exercise 9. Watch the video for how the numbers are written. Then write your own in the space provided, and pronounce them aloud as you write them.

درس چهار: شغل شما چیست؟ What Do You Do?

۱۱ ۱۲ ۱۳ ۱۴ ۱۵

۱۶ ۱۷ ۱۸ ۱۹ ۲۰

Exercise 10. Class Activity

With a partner, take turns counting from 10 to 20 in intervals of 2 and 3 and then from 1 to 20 in intervals of 5.

Exercise 11. Answer the following questions using Persian numbers.

How many?
Eggs in a dozen _____
Days in a week _____
Months in a year _____
Fingers and toes on the human body _____

🎧 **Exercise 12.** Listen to the audio and circle the number you hear in each set.

1. ۱۶, ۱۵, ۱۴
2. ۱۷, ۱۸, ۱۹
3. ۱۳, ۱۲, ۱۱
4. ۶, ۷, ۸
5. ۱۴, ۱۹, ۱۶
6. ۲۰, ۱۸, ۱۱
7. ۵, ۶, ۴
8. ۱۲, ۱۴, ۱۳

🎧 **Exercise 13.** Listen and practice. Notice the pronunciation.

۱. یک - یازدَه   ۲. دو - دوازدَه   ۳. سه - سیزدَه
۴. چَهار - چَهاردَه   ۵. پَنج - پانزدَه   ۶. شش - شانزدَه
۷. هفت - هفدَه   ۸. هشت - هجدَه   ۹. نُه - نوزدَه

🎧 **Exercise 14. Dictation:** Listen to the words dictated to you and write them in the space provided.

۱. _____   ۲. _____
۳. _____   ۴. _____
۵. _____   ۶. _____
۷. _____   ۸. _____
۹. _____   ۱۰. _____
۱۱. _____   ۱۲. _____

C. The Letter (ṭā) ط

The letter *ṭā* is a voiceless stop (a sound made by completely blocking the flow of air and then releasing it) that has the same pronunciation as ت. This letter is written in two strokes. First, an oval shape above the line (similar to ص and ض) is written, followed by a vertical line that starts at the top and connects to the oval shape. *Ṭā* shares a similar shape in the initial and freestanding positions, as it does in the medial and final positions. It connects to a following letter in the initial position; however, in the medial position, it can connect from both sides. In the final position, it can only connect to a preceding letter. There are four different forms of this letter shown in the following table. However, as explained earlier, and due to the similarities of the initial and freestanding and the medial and final, only the two main forms are practiced.

Freestanding	Final	Medial	Initial
ط	ط	ط	ط

🎥 **Exercise 15.** Watch the video for how the shapes of the letter ط is written. Trace the model letter, and then practice writing your own in the space provided and pronounce it aloud.

D. The Letter (ẓā) ظ

The letter *ẓā*, a voiced fricative consonant, has the same sound as ز and ض, and a similar shape to ط except that it has one dot above. There are four different forms of this letter, and its connectivity is the same as ط, as shown in the table that follows.

Freestanding	Final	Medial	Initial
ظ	ظ	ظ	ظ

🎥 **Exercise 16.** Watch the video for how the shapes of the letter ظ are written. Trace the model letter, and then practice writing your own in the space provided and pronounce it aloud.

درس چهار: شغل شما چیست؟ What Do You Do?

Exercise 17. Listen to the following words and repeat.

| ۴. چطور | ۳. حَیاط | ۲. طوطی | ۱. طَناب |
| ۸. مَنظور | ۷. نَظَر | ۶. ناظِم | ۵. ظُهر |

Exercise 18. Join the letters in each set to form words.

۱. چ + ـَ + ط + و + ر ← ....

۲. ظ + ـُ + ه + ر ← ....

۳. ط + و + ط + ی ← ....

۴. ط + ا + و + س ← ....

۵. ط + ـَ + ن + ا + ب ← ....

۶. ح + ـَ + ی + ا + ط ← ....

۷. ن + ا + ظ + ـِ + م ← ....

۸. ن + ـَ + ظ + ـَ + ر ← ....

۹. م + ـَ + ن + ظ + و + ر ← ....

Exercise 19. Read the following words. Remember to read from right to left.

۳. چطور	۲. طوطی	۱. طَناب
۶. مَربوط	۵. رابط	۴. رَبط
۹. طاووس	۸. مُحیط	۷. حَیاط
۱۲. مُنتَظِر	۱۱. ناظِم	۱۰. ظُهر
۱۵. مُواظِب	۱۴. مَنظور	۱۳. نَظَر

74 What Do You Do? ‏درس چهار: شغل شما چیست؟

Exercise 20. Practice writing the following words in the space provided.

طَناب   طَناب

طوطی   طوطی

چِطور   چطور

حَیاط   حَیاط

رَبط   رَبط

نَظَر   نَظَر

ظُهر   ظُهر

🎧 **Exercise 21. Dictation:** Listen to the words dictated to you and write them in the space provided.

۱. _____   ۲. _____
۳. _____   ۴. _____
۵. _____   ۶. _____
۷. _____   ۸. _____
۹. _____   ۱۰. _____
۱۱. _____ ۱۲. _____

E. The Letter ('eyn) ع

The letter *'eyn* is a glottal stop (a speech sound made by completely closing and then opening your glottis) that represents the sound *[']*. It is written with one stroke and has four different forms. In its initial and freestanding positions, there are two loops, the top loop that sits on the line and the larger loop that resembles the English letter *C* below the line. In the medial and final positions, the top is a closed loop. The letter ع connects to a following letter in the initial position. In the medial position, it can connect from both sides, and in the final position, it can only connect to a preceding letter.

Freestanding	Final	Medial	Initial
ع	ع	ع	ع

🎥 **Exercise 22.** Watch the video for how the shapes of the letter ع are written. Trace the model letter, and then practice writing your own in the space provided and pronounce it aloud.

F. The Letter (gheyn) غ

The letter *gheyn* has no equivalent in English; it is produced further back in the throat compared to English *[g]* in *gate*. This letter is written similarly to ع except that it has one dot above the top loop. Its connectivity is the same as ع, as shown in the following table.

Freestanding	Final	Medial	Initial
غ	غ	غ	غ

🎥 **Exercise 23.** Watch the video for how the shapes of the letter غ are written. Trace the model letter, and then practice writing your own in the space provided and pronounce it aloud.

درس چهار: شغل شما چیست؟ What Do You Do?

🎧 **Exercise 24.** You will hear nine words that contain either ع or غ. As you listen, determine whether each word has ع or غ and then circle it.

۳. ع/ غ	۲. غ/ ع	۱. ع/ غ
۶. غ/ ع	۵. ع/ غ	۴. ع/ غ
۹. ع/ غ	۸. غ/ ع	۷. ع/ غ

🎧 **Exercise 25.** Listen to the following words and repeat.

۴. شُروع	۳. یَعنی	۲. عَمو	۱. ساعَت
۸. جیغ	۷. جُغد	۶. مُرغابی	۵. مُرغ

Exercise 26. Join the letters in each set to form words.

1. ع + َ + م + و → ....

2. ع + ِ + ی + د → ....

3. ش + ِ + ع + ر → ....

4. ش + ُ + ر + و + ع → ....

5. ج + َ + م + ع → ....

6. ج + ُ + غ + د → ....

What Do You Do? درس چهار: شغل شما چیست؟

7. غ + ر + ـُـ + م → ....

8. س + ا + ع + ـَـ + ت → ....

9. ی + ـَـ + ع + ن + ی → ....

10. ت+ـَـ + ع + ط + ی + ل → ....

11. ب + ـَـ + ع + د → ....

Exercise 27. Read the following words. Remember to read from right to left.

۱. ساعَت	۲. عید	۳. عَمو
۴. بَعد	۵. جَمع	۶. شَمع
۷. شعر	۸. شُروع	۹. موضوع
۱۰. شاعر	۱۱. غایب	۱۲. تَعطیل
۱۳. مُرغابی	۱۴. جُغَد	۱۵. جیغ
۱۶. باغ	۱۷. مُرغ	۱۸. دوغ
۱۹. یَعنی	۲۰. عَرَبِستان	۲۱. اَفغانِستان

🎧 **Exercise 28.** You will hear nine words that may contain the sound *[gh]*. As you listen to each word, circle **yes** if you the sound *[gh]* and **no** if you do not.

1. yes no	2. yes no	3. yes no
4. yes no	5. yes no	6. yes no
7. yes no	8. yes no	9. yes no

Exercise 29. Practice writing the following words in the space provided.

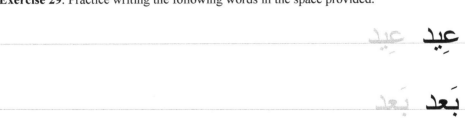

شُروع شُروع شُروع

جَمع جَمع جَمع

جُغد جُغد جُغد

مُرغ مُرغ مُرغ

عَمو عَمو عَمو

تَعطیل تَعطیل تَعطیل

🎧 **Exercise 30. Dictation:** Listen to the words dictated to you and write them in the space provided.

۱. _____		۲. _____	
۳. _____		۴. _____	
۵. _____		۶. _____	
۷. _____		۸. _____	
۹. _____		۱۰. _____	
۱۱. _____		۱۲. _____	

🎧 **Exercise 31.** Listen to the pronunciation of the following words and write their short vowel signs.

۱. مریض	۲. مواظب	۳. چطور	۴. عمو
۵. صبح	۶. عید	۷. مرغ	۸. حیاط

Exercise 32. Write the letters of the following words in the space provided.

مَعنی ـ ـ ـ ـ
صُحبَت ـ ـ ـ ـ
موضوع ـ ـ ـ ـ

درس چهار: شغل شما چیست؟ What Do You Do?

🎧 **Exercise 33.** For each number below, you will hear three words. Two of the words will be the same. Write **a** if you hear the first one as different, **b** if the second, or **c** if you hear the third one as different.

1. _____ 2. _____ 3. _____
4. _____ 5. _____ 6. _____

Exercise 34. Write six words that contain one of the following letters ص ض ط ظ ع غ in the space provided.

1. _____ 2. _____ 3. _____
4. _____ 5. _____ 6. _____

🎧 **Exercise 35. Dictation:** Listen to the words dictated to you and write them in the space provided.

1. _____ 2. _____
3. _____ 4. _____
5. _____ 6. _____
7. _____ 8. _____
9. _____ 10. _____
11. _____ 12. _____

Exercise 36. Complete the following words by filling out the missing letter indicated by the space between the letters. The missing letters are ص ض ط ظ ع غ ه. Add diacritics as needed.

۱. حَیا...   ۲. ...بحانَ   ۳. خانَ...   ۴. ...ید   ۵. مو...وع
۶. مَخ...و...   ۷. یَ...نی   ۸. د...   ۹. مُر...   ۱۰. سا...ت

Exercise 37. Write words for each set of letters, as in the example.

/t/	ت	تاب	_____
	ط	طَناب	_____
/s/	س	_____	_____
	ص	_____	_____
/z/	ز	_____	_____
	ض	_____	_____
	ظ	_____	_____

G. The Letter (lām) ل

The sound of the letter *lām* resembles the English *[l]* in *last*. In the final and freestanding positions, the forms are similar to ک but lower below the line and without the slash. The initial and medial positions, however, are to some degree similar to the connecting *alef*. There are four different forms of this letter, as shown in the table that follows. This letter connects to a following letter in the initial position, but in the medial position, it can connect from both sides. In the final position, it can only connect to a preceding letter.

Freestanding	Final	Medial	Initial
ل	ـل	ـلـ	لـ

Exercise 38. Watch the video for how the shapes of the letter ل are written. Then practice writing your own in the space provided and pronounce it aloud.

Important Note: When *alef* follows *lām*, the combination of the two is written as *alef* embedded in *lām*. This combination is written in two strokes, first, *lām* and then *alef* is added starting from the top.

Freestanding	Connecting
لا	ـلا

Exercise 39. Trace the model letters, and then write your own letter in the space provided.

81 درس چهار: شغل شما چیست؟ What Do You Do?

Exercise 40. Join the letters in each set to form words.

1. س + ا + ل ← ....
2. سَ + ل + ا + م ← ....
3. لِ + ب + ا + س ← ....
4. شُ + ل + و + ا + ر ← ....
5. شُ + غ + ل ← ....
6. پُ + ل + ی + س ← ....
7. لَ + ن + دَ + ن ← ....
8. ا + ل + م + ا + ن ← ....
9. جِ + ا + ل + ب ← ....
10. ا + ی + ت + ا + ل + ی + ا ← ....

Exercise 41. Read the following words. Remember to read from right to left.

۱. لَب	۲. لَبخَند	۳. خوشحال
۴. پول	۵. هُتل	۶. بلیت
۷. جالب	۸. عالی	۹. تَنبَل
۱۰. سَلام	۱۱. سالم	۱۲. سَلامَتی
۱۳. سال	۱۴. لباس	۱۵. لیوان
۱۶. شُغل	۱۷. پُلیس	۱۸. خَلَبان
۱۹. لَندَن	۲۰. آلمان	۲۱. ایتالیا

درس چهار: شغل شما چیست؟ What Do You Do?

Exercise 42. Circle the misspelled word in each set, and write it correctly in the space provided.

تاب	تَناب	طوطی	_____
ریاضی	سَبزی	سُبح بِخیر	_____
حازر	عِید	صُحبَت	_____
تَهطیل	مُرغ	مَریض	_____

Exercise 43. Practice writing the following words in the space provided.

سَلام سَلام _____

سال سال _____

لِباس لِباس _____

شُغل شُغل _____

عالی عالی _____

پُلیس پُلیس _____

خوشحال خوشحال _____

🎧 **Exercise 44. Dictation:** Listen to the words dictated to you and write them in the space provided.

۲. _____	۱. _____
۴. _____	۳. _____
۶. _____	۵. _____
۸. _____	۷. _____
۱۰. _____	۹. _____
۱۲. _____	۱۱. _____

Exercise 45. Identify the letters ل غ ع ظ ط ض ص by circling them in the following:

عمو علی در باغش سه مرغابی، هفت غاز و ده مرغ دارد.
حیاط خانه اش در طبقه ی اول و پر از درخت بلوط است.
عمو علی می گوید آلبالو ، آلو
گیلاس و لیمو در سالاد با بلال و لوبیا بسیار جالب
و خوشمزه است.
تَبلیغات مجموعه فیلمهای صوتی و تصویری
صورت زیبای ظاهر هیچ نیست
لی لی به لالای کسی گذاشتن

2 Grammar

Short Form of the Verb "To Be"

In Lesson Three, you learned about the verb "to be" and its conjugation, which is considered the long forms of the verb "to be." In this lesson, you will learn the short forms. The short forms in the singular and plural are mainly verb endings except for the third-person singular as indicated in the following chart.

Short Form of the Verb "To Be" بودَن

We are	/-im/ ...یم		I am	/-am/ ...م
You are (pl)	/-id/ ...ید		You are	/-i/ ...ی
They are	/-and/ ...نَد		S/he is	/ast/ أست

All the short forms are joined to a preceding word except for أست. For the third-person singular (او), there is no short form. Thus, أست is written as a separate word.

ما خوشحالیم We are happy	مَن خوشحالَم I am happy
شُما خوشحالید You are happy (pl)	تو خوشحالی You are happy
آنها خوشحالَند They are happy	او خوشحال اَست S/he is happy

Some Points about the Short Form of "To Be"

1. If the preceding word ends in ه /e/, an *alef* is inserted before the short form except for the third-person singular:

او خَسته اَست	تو خَسته ای	مَن خَسته ام
/khaste ast/ He/ she is tired	/khastei/ You are tired	/khasteam/ I am tired
آنها خَسته آند	شُما خَسته اید	ما خَسته ایم
/khasteand/ They are tired	/khasteid/ You are tired (pl)	/khasteim/ We are tired

2. If the preceding word ends in ا /ā/ and/or و /u/, a *ye* is inserted before the short form except for the third-person singular:

او دانشجو است	تو دانشجویی	مَن دانشجویَم
/dāneshju ast/ He/she is a student	/dāneshjui/ You are a student	/dāneshjuyam/ I am a student
آنها دانشجویَند	شُما دانشجویید	ما دانشجوییم
/dāneshjuyand/ They are students	/dāneshjuid/ You are students (pl)	/dāneshjūim/ We are students

3. If the preceding word ends in ی /i/, it is connected to the short form, except for the third-person singular:

او ایرانی است	تو ایرانیی	مَن ایرانیَم
/irāni ast/ He/she is Iranian	/irānii/ You are Iranian	/irāniam/ I am Iranian
آنها ایرانیَند	شُما ایرانیید	ما ایرانییم
/irāniyand/ They are Iranians	/irāniid/ You are Iranians (pl)	/irāniim/ We are Iranians

4. The short form can be written separately with an inserted *alef* after و /u/ and ی /i/ as well:

مَن ایرانی آم	مَن دانشجو آم
/irāniam/ I am Iranian	/dāneshjuam/ I am a student

5. است may lose the *alef* after a word that ends in a long vowel:

دانشجوست	اینجاست	چیست
/dāneshjust/ He/she is a student	/injāst/ He/she is here	/chist/ What is it

6. In spoken Persian, است is pronounced /e/ when it is preceded by a word ending in a consonant:

/khube/ It's good   /khub ast/ It's good

7. Also, in spoken Persian, the short forms of the second- and third-person plural, /-ید/ and /-ند/, lose the د:

خوبید /khubid/ ⟵ خوبین /khubin/
You're good (pl)

خوبَند /khuband/ ⟵ خوبَن /khuban/
They're good

The Negation

The short forms do not have a negative form. The only negative forms that are used for the verb "to be" in both long and short forms are the forms with نیست that you learned in the previous lesson.

We are not /nistim/ نیستیم	I am not /nistam/ نیستم
You are not (pl.) /nistid/ نیستید	You are not /nisti/ نیستی
They are not /nistand/ نیستند	S/he/it is not /nist/ نیست

Exercise 46. Change the verbs of the following sentences to the short form and write them in the space provided.

۱. او ایرانی است.
۲. ما دانشجو هستیم.
۳. شما مُهَندِس هستید؟
۴. آنها تهرانی نیستند.

Exercise 47. Put the following set of words into order and write them in the space provided.

۱. خَسته – مَن – هَستَم
۲. پدَر – او – من – اَست – دوست
۳. اُو – اِسمِ – سینا – بَرادَر – اَست
۴. مینا – اُستاد – نیست – مادر

Exercise 48. Change to the spoken form.

۱. این دوستِ من ژوبین است.
۲. تو پَرَستار هستی؟
۳. آنها خوشحال هستَند؟
۴. آقای نادِری مُعلِم است.

Exercise 49. Change to the long form of "to be."

۱. تو خوبی؟
۲. شما چطورید؟
۳. من شاعِرَم.
۴. آنها نویسنده اَند.

Ezāfe

The Persian *ezāfe* construction is a vowel /-e/ that appears between a noun and its modifier. It shows the relationship of a noun to a following word or words. *ezāfe* is pronounced /-e/ after words that end in consonants, and /-ye/ after words that end in long vowels.

Ezafe *is added to*

a. a noun followed by one or more modifiers:

Mina's daughter	/dokhtare minā/	دُختَرِ مینا
Persian language book	/ketābe zabāne fārsi/	کتابِ زبانِ فارسی
my pencil	/medāde man/	مدادِ مَن
big city	/shahre bozorg/	شَهرِ بُزرگ

b. a noun followed by proper names of people, universities, streets, cities, and countries:

Mrs. Naderi	/khānume nāderi/	خانمِ نادری
Tehran University	/dāneshgāhe tehrān/	دانشگاهِ تهران
Fereshteh Street	/khiyābāne fereshte/	خیابانِ فرشته
(city of) Shiraz	/shahre shirāz/	شَهرِ شیراز
(country of) Iran	/keshvare irān/	کِشوَرِ ایران

c. a noun that ends in (ا) /ā/ or (و) /u/, is written as ی and pronounced /ye/:

Mr. Naderi	/āqāye nāderi/	آقای نادری
lazy (college) student	/daneshjuye tanbal/	دانشجوی تنبل

d. a noun that ends in (ه) /e/, is written as ی, and is pronounced /ye/:

our house	/khāneye mā/	خانه ی ما
good children	/bachehāye khub/	بچه ی خوب

Exercise 50. Listen to the following phrases with *ezafe* and repeat.

دوستِ ما	مادَرِ بیتا	اُستادِ فارسی
مُهندسِ شیمی	حَیاطِ آنها	شَهرِ زیبا

Exercise 51. Indicate whether *ezafe* in the following is /e/ or /ye/.

آسمانِ آبی	خانهِ اُمید	دُخترِ خانمِ احمَدی
بچهِ خوب	عیدِ نوروز	دانِشجوِ خَسته

درس چهار: شغل شما چیست؟ What Do You Do?

🎧 **Exercise 52. Dictation:** Listen to the sentences and write them in the space provided.

۱. _____
۲. _____
۳. _____
۴. _____
۵. _____
۶. _____
۷. _____

3 Listening and Conversation

Asking Someone What Job They Do and Talking About What Job You Do

There are different ways to ask someone what job they have or what their occupation is. For example:

/shoghle shomā chiye/ (What is your occupation?)	شُغلِ شُما چیه؟
/shomā che kāreid/ (What do you do?)	شُما چه کاره اید؟
/kāre shomā chist/ (What is your job?)	کارِ شما چیست؟
/shomā che kār mikonid/ (What do you do?)	شُما چه کار می کُنید؟

To talk about what your occupation is, you use the first-person singular personal pronoun مَن, followed by an occupation and the verb "to be," as illustrated in the example shown.

/man dāneshju hastam/ (I am a college student)	مَن دانشجو هَستَم

🎧 **Exercise 53.** Listen to the pronunciation of the following list of jobs and repeat.

doctor	دُکتُر	cook	آشپَز
psychologist	روانشناس	professor	اُستاد
soldier	سَرباز	nurse	پَرستار
poet	شاعِر	police	پُلیس
translator	مُترجِم	accountant	حِسابدار
teacher	مُعَلِّم	pilot	خَلَبان
engineer	مُهَندِس	pharmacist	داروساز
writer	نویسَنده	scientist	دانشمَند
artist	هُنَرمَند	college student	دانشجو

88 What Do You Do? درس چهار: شغل شما چیست؟

🎧 **Exercise 54.**

A. Listen to the audio and practice each line several times. Be prepared to hold a similar conversation in class with your classmates.
B. Listen to the audio again and answer the questions.

۱. شُغلِ مَهیار چیه؟
۲. شُغلِ آقای نادِری چیه؟
۳. شُغلِ خانمِ نادِری چیه؟

_____
_____
_____

Exercise 55. Match the jobs with the pictures. Write the corresponding letter under each picture.

الف. خَلَبان	ب. دُکتُر	پ. آشپَز
ت. اُستاد	ث. هُنَرمَند	ج. پَرِستار
چ. دانشجو	ح. داروساز	خ. سَرباز

درس چهار: شغل شما چیست؟ What Do You Do?

🎧 **Exercise 56.**

A. Listen to the audio and practice each line several times. Be prepared to hold a similar conversation in class with your classmates.
B. Listen to the audio again and fill in the blanks.

- مینا جان، این آرشه. اون _____ امیره.
- سلام. خوشوقتم.
- مینا خانم، شما _____ هستین؟
- بله ، من _____ هستم. شما چی _____؟
- من _____ . _____ من _____
- شما پسر خانم نادری _____ نیستین؟
- بله ، خانمِ نادری مادرِ مَنه.
- خانم نادری _____ من هستن.
- مینا خانم، مادر شما هم _____ _____ هستن؟
- نه، مادرِ من _____ .

C. Listen to the dialogue again. Check True or False.

True	False	
____	____	۱. امیر دوست آرش است
____	____	۲. مینا مُعَلِم اَست
____	____	۳. خانم نادری روانشناس است
____	____	۴. مادرِ مینا استاد نیست

🎧 **Exercise 57.**

A. Listen to the audio and practice each line several times. Be prepared to hold a similar conversation in class with your classmates.
B. Listen to the audio again as the four people talk about their jobs. Complete the chart with the correct job and adjective for each person.

What Do You Do? درس چهار: شغل شما چیست؟

What do they do	Adjective	
....	....	۱. نازی
....	....	۲. آرمان
....	....	۳. علی
....	....	۴. خانم تهرانی

Exercise 58. Class Activity

Dictation: Work with a partner, where one of you will be Student 1 and the other Student 2 giving each other a dictation. Student 1 would be reading List A and Student 2 would be reading List B.

Step 1: Student 1 covers up List B.
Step 2: Student 1 spells aloud the words from List A for Student 2 to write down.
Step 3: Student 2 writes down the words.
Step 4: Student 2 spells aloud the words from List B as Student 1 writes them down.

List A	List B
خَلَبان	شُغل
پُلیس	دانِشجو
پَرستار	آشپز
دانِشمَند	مُهَندِس
شاعِر	لَندَن
ایتالیا	مِصر
آلمان	صُبح
ساعَت	عَمو
شُروع	چِطور
تَعطیل	بَعد

Exercise 59. Look at the pictures and write a sentence indicating each person's job.

Example:

	این زَن آشپَز است. (این زَن آشپَزه.)

درس چهار: شغل شما چیست؟ What Do You Do?

Exercise 60. Class Activity

Ask three classmates about their jobs (or their friends or family members' jobs). Then tell the class.

Exercise 61. Class Activity.

With two classmates, choose a job for each person and make sentences.

١. مَریم
٢. سینا
٣. اُمید
٤. آقای نادری

_____

_____

_____

_____

🎧 Listening and Conversation Vocabulary

The following is a list of vocabulary terms related to the conversations. The list includes the spoken as well as the written/formal, form of the vocabulary; their meaning; and their pronunciation using transliteration. The vocabulary terms are organized according to their appearance in the conversations.

Meaning	Transliteration	Written/Formal	Spoken/Colloquial
Mr./Sir	āqā	آقا	آقا
Mrs./Lady	khānum	خانُم	خانوم
History	tārikh	تاریخ	تاریخ
Excellent	ā'li	عالی	عالی
Beautiful	zibā	زیبا	زیبا

Vocabulary Review Chart

English	Pronunciation	Persian
Professor	ostād	اُستاد
Chef, cook	āshpaz	آشپَز
Next, then	ba'd	بَعد
Nurse	parastār	پَرَستار
Police	polis	پُلیس
Money	pul	پول
Holiday, closed, off	ta'til	تَعطیل

English	Pronunciation	Persian
How	chetor	چِطور
Courtyard	hayāt	حَیاط
Pilot	khalabān	خَلَبان
Happy	khoshhāl	خوشحال
Yogurt drink	dogh	دوغ
Math	riyāzi	ریاضی
Hello	salām	سَلام
Beginning, start	shoru'	شُروع
Job, occupation,	shoql	شُغل
Good morning	sobh bekheyr	صُبح بِخیر
Breakfast	sobhāne	صُبحانه
Face	sorat	صورَت
Pink	sorati	صورَتی
Parrot	tuti	طوطی
Noon	zohr	ظُهر
Paternal uncle	amu	عَمو
Celebration	eyd	عید
Glass	livān	لیوان
Special	makhsus	مَخصوص
Sick	mariz	مَریض
Chicken	morq	مُرغ
Hotel	hotel	هُتِل

Lesson 5

WHERE ARE YOU FROM? درس پنج: اهل کجایی؟

In this lesson you will learn:

- Letters

  ف ق
  ک گ

- Grammar
  - The Plural
  - Adjectival ی /ye/

- Listening and Conversation
  - Talking About One's Nationality
  - Asking Where Someone Is From

---

1 Letters

A. The Letter (fe) ف

The letter *fe* is pronounced *[f]* similar to the English letter *f*, as in the word *fast*. This letter is written with one stroke starting with the top loop, continuing on the line and finishing just a little above the line with one dot. There are four different forms of this letter, where the final and freestanding are similar. The letter *fe* connects to a following letter in the initial position, but in the medial position, it can connect from both sides. In the final position, it can only connect to a preceding letter.

درس پنج: اهل کجایی؟ Where Are You From?

Freestanding	Final	Medial	Initial
ف	ـف	ـفـ	فـ

📹 **Exercise 1.** Watch the video for how the shapes of the letter ف are written. Trace the model letter, and then practice writing your own in the space provided and pronounce it aloud.

B. *The Letter* (qāf) ق

In Persian, the letter *qāf* is pronounced the same as غ , and there is no English equivalent for it. Although the letter *qāf* is different in sound from ف, in form, the initial and medial positions look similar except for the number of dots, as the letter *qāf* has two dots. In the final and freestanding positions, unlike ف, following the top loop, there's a curve below the line. The connectivity of the letter *qāf* is the same as ف, as in the initial position, it connects to a following letter, but in the medial position, it can connect from both sides. In the final position, it can only connect to a preceding letter.

Freestanding	Final	Medial	Initial
ق	ـق	ـقـ	قـ

📹 **Exercise 2.** Watch the video for how the shapes of the letter ق are written. Trace the model letter, and then practice writing your own in the space provided and pronounce it aloud.

درس پنج: اهل کجایی؟ Where Are You From?

ق ق ق

ــق ــق ــق

ق ق

ق ق ق

Exercise 3. Listen to the following words and repeat.

۴. آفَرین	۳. آفتاب	۲. بَرف	۱. فَردا
۸. عَراق	۷. قَطَر	۶. قَطار	۵. قایق
۱۲. قَدیمی	۱۱. قَوی	۱۰. سُفره	۹. سَفیر

Exercise 4. Join the letters in each set to form words.

1. ب + ـَ + ر + ف ← ....
2. ف + ـَ + ر + ش ← ....
3. ق + ـَ + ن + د ← ....
4. ف + ـَ + ر + ا + ن + س + ه ← ....
5. ق + ا + ی + ـِ + ق ← ....
6. ق + ا + ش + ـُ + ق ← ....
7. ب + ـُ + ش + ق + ا + ب ← ....
8. ا + ف + ت + ا + ب ← ....
9. ق + ـِ + ر + م + ـِ + ز ← ....
11. س + ـُ + ر + ف + ه ← ....
12. س + ـِ + ف + ی + د ← ....
13. ف + ا + ر + س + ی ← ....

درس پنج: اهل کجایی؟ Where Are You From?

Exercise 5. Read the following words. Remember to read from right to left.

۳. قَوی	۲. قَند	۱. قَهوه
۶. قَطَر	۵. فوتبال	۴. عَراق
۹. قرمز	۸. فَرش	۷. قالی
۱۲. قَدیمی	۱۱. قایق	۱۰. مَشق
۱۵. دَفتَر	۱۴. فَرزاد	۱۳. فَردا
۱۸. آفَرین	۱۷. قَندان	۱۶. فَندُق
۲۱. سُفره	۲۰. سَفیر	۱۹. سَفَر
۲۴. چاقو	۲۳. بُشقاب	۲۲. قاشُق

🎧 **Exercise 6.** You will hear nine words that may contain the sound *[f]*. As you listen to each word, circle **yes** if you hear the sound *[f]*, and circle **no** if you do not.

1. yes no   2. yes no   3. yes no
4. yes no   5. yes no   6. yes no
7. yes no   8. yes no   9. yes no

Exercise 7. Practice writing the following words in the space provided.

آقا آقا _____

اُتاق اُتاق _____

دَفتَر دَفتَر _____

فَردا فَردا _____

فارسی فارسی _____

قاشُق قاشُق _____

بُشقاب بُشقاب _____

98 Where Are You From? درس پنج: اهل کجایی؟

🎧 **Exercise 8. Dictation:** Listen to the words dictated to you and write them in the space provided.

_____ .۲   _____ .۱

_____ .۴   _____ .۳

_____ .۶   _____ .۵

_____ .۸   _____ .۷

_____ .۱۰   _____ .۹

_____ .۱۲   _____ .۱۱

C. The Letter (kāf) ک

The letter *(kāf)* resembles the English sound *[k]* as in the word *cat*. It has four forms, and it is written in two strokes. Start above the line, going down as you make an angle to the right and continue on the line. Next, draw a slanted line connected to the body of the letter. In the initial and medial positions, the main body of the letter is drawn shorter than the other two positions. This letter connects to a following letter in the initial position, and in the medial position, it connects from both sides. In the final position, it can only connect to a preceding letter.

Freestanding	Final	Medial	Initial
ک	ک	ک	ک

Exercise 9. Watch the video for how the shapes of the letter ک are written. Trace the model letter, then practice writing your own in the space provided and pronounce it aloud.

D. The Letter (gāf) گ

The letter *gāf* corresponds to the English sound *[g]* as in the word *gain*. It is written similarly to ک except that it takes two strokes on top. Thus, *gāf* is written in three strokes. After the body of the letter and the slanted line are drawn, a second but slightly shorter slanted line is added. *Gāf* has four different forms, and its connectivity is the same as ک, as shown in the following table.

Freestanding	Final	Medial	Initial
گ	ـگ	ـگـ	گـ

Exercise 10. Watch the video for how the shapes of the letter ک are written. Trace the model letter, and then practice writing your own in the space provided below and pronounce it aloud.

Exercise 11. Listen to the following words and repeat.

۴. کُت	۳. کفش	۲. کیف	۱. کتاب
۸. بُزُرگ	۷. گُل	۶. انگُشت	۵. گوش

Exercise 12. You will hear nine words that may contain the sound *[k]*. As you listen to each word, circle **yes** if you hear the sound *[k]* and **no** if you do not.

1.	yes	no	2.	yes	no	3.	yes	no
4.	yes	no	5.	yes	no	6.	yes	no
7.	yes	no	8.	yes	no	9.	yes	no

Exercise 13. Read the following words. Remember to read from right to left.

۳. کِلاس	۲. کِتاب	۱. یِک
۶. می کُنَم	۵. زِندِگی	۴. گَرم
۹. می گویَم	۸. پِدَر بُزُرگ	۷. مادَر بُزُرگ
۱۲. بُزُرگ	۱۱. قَشنگ	۱۰. فُروشگاه
۱۵. دُکتُر	۱۴. کارمَند	۱۳. کار
۱۸. کُجا	۱۷. کَشتی	۱۶. تاکسی
۲۱. کوچِک	۲۰. نَزدیک	۱۹. کِشوَر
۲۴. کُردِستان	۲۳. کاشان	۲۲. کِرمان
۲۷. آمریکا	۲۶. کانادا	۲۵. اِنگِلیس
۳۰. پاکِستان	۲۹. مِکزیک	۲۸. نیویورک

🎧 **Exercise 14.** You will hear nine words that contain either ق or گ. As you listen, determine whether each word has ق or گ and circle the letter.

۳. ق / گ	۲. گ / ق	۱. ق / گ
۶. گ / ق	۵. ق / گ	۴. گ / ق
۹. ق / گ	۸. گ / ق	۷. ق / گ

Exercise 15. Join the letters in each set to form words.

درس پنج: اهل کجایی؟ Where Are You From?

۱. س + ا + ل + ِ + ک → ....
۲. ش + ف + َ + ک → ....
۳. م + ا + ل + َ + س → ....
۴. ا + ی + ل + ا + ت+ی +ا → ....
۵. ا + د + ا + ن + ا + ک → ....
۶. ا + ج + ُ + ک → ....
۷. س+ی +ل+ِ+گ+ن + ِ → ....
۸. ا + ک+ی + ر + م + ا → ....
۹. ا + ل + م + ا + ن → ....
۱۱. ف+و+ ت + ب + ا + ل → ....
۱۲. ب + ُ + ز + ُ + ر+ گ → ....
۱۳. د + ُ + ک + ُ + ت + ُ + ر → ....

Exercise 16. Practice writing the following words in the space provided.

سَلام سَلام ....

کِلاس کِلاس ....

کِتاب کِتاب ....

کیف کیف ....

فُروشگاه فُروشگاه ....

کِشَور کِشَور ....

آمریکا آمریکا ....

آلمان آلمان ....

Exercise 17. Make words. The letter in the circle added to the beginning of the content of each of the four boxes makes a word. Write the words you make in the space provided and add diacritical marks as needed. Practice pronouncing each word.

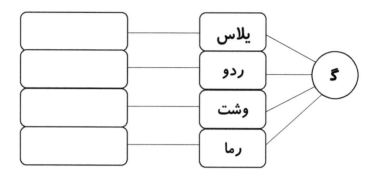

Exercise 18. Write two words with the forms of the letters given in the following table.

		ع ء
_____	_____	ف ف
_____	_____	ق ق
_____	_____	

Exercise 19. Find examples of the word in the right column from among the list of words given in the left column. Circle your answer.

List of Words	Word
دوست بست نیست است هست بیست	نیست
حانم حاتم خانم جانم خانم دانم	خانم
پوری قوری شوری فوری قوری جوری	قوری
ضوابط روابط ربط ضبط رابط زبط	ربط

Exercise 20. For each number in the table, you will hear three words. Two of the words will be the same. Write **a** if you hear the first one as different, **b** if the second, or **c** if you hear the third one as different.

Where Are You From? درس پنج: اهل کجایی؟

1. _____ 2. _____ 3. _____
4. _____ 5. _____ 6. _____

🎧 **Exercise 21. Dictation:** Listen to the words dictated to you and write them in the space that follows.

1. _____   2. _____
3. _____   4. _____
5. _____   6. _____
7. _____   8. _____
9. _____   10. _____
11. _____ 12. _____

Exercise22. Identify the letters ف ق ک گ and personal pronouns by circling them in the following:

خُدا گَر زِ حِکمَت بِبَندد دری

ز رَحمَت گُشاید دَر دیگری

مادر بزرگ و پدر بزرگ کاوه و گلاره را به گردش بردند. پدر به کبابهای روی کباب پز با نمکدان نمک زد. دیروز وقتی برف بارید، فریبا ،فریده و فرزاد آدم برفی درست کردند. وقتی خواهرم مسابقه می دهد او را تشویق می کنم.
تاجیکستان، ازبکستان، قزاقزستان و قرقیزستان از اعضای اصلی سازمان همکاری شانگهای هستند. در حالی که پاکستان، افغانستان و مغولستان جزو کشورهای ناظر هستند.

2 Grammar

The Plural

In Persian, there are two plural markers/suffixes that can be added to nouns to change them from singular to plural: ها /ha/ and ان /an/. ها /ha/ can be added to all nouns, while ان /an/ is added to animate nouns. Both of these plural markers can be connected to the nouns they modify. They can also be written separately.

(girls)	دُختران	⇐	دُختر	(watches)	ساعتها ⇐ ساعت
(boys)	پسران	⇐	پسر	(tables)	میزها ⇐ میز
(men)	مَردان	⇐	مَرد	(pencils)	مِدادها ⇐ مِداد
(women)	زَنان	⇐	زَن	(computers)	کامپیوترها ⇐ کامپیوتِر

If a noun ends in (ه) /e/, the plural suffix is not connected to the noun:

houses	/khānehā/	خانه ها
children	/bachehā/	بچه ها

If a noun ends in (ا) /ā/ or (و) /u/, the plural suffix becomes یان /yān/:

gentlemen	/āqāyān/	آقایان
college students	/dāneshjuyān/	دانشجویان

Exercise 23. Write the plural form(s) of the following nouns.

۹. بُشقاب _____		۱. کِتاب _____	
۱۰. قاشُق _____		۲. کِلاس _____	
۱۱. تِلِفُن _____		۳. دُکتُر _____	
۱۲. کَباب _____		۴. کارمَند _____	
۱۳. دُختَر _____		۵. ژاکت _____	
۱۴. بَرادَر _____		۶. گُل _____	
۱۵. پدَر _____		۷. دِرَخت _____	
۱۶. مادَر _____		۸. دَست _____	

🎧 **Exercise 24. Dictation:** Listen to the sentences you hear and write them in the space provided.

Where Are You From? درس پنج: اهل کجایی؟

۱. _____
۲. _____
۳. _____
۴. _____
۵. _____
۶. _____
۷. _____
۸. _____
۹. _____
۱۰. _____

Adjectival ی /-ye/

In Lesson 4, you learned that after words that end in long vowels, *ezāfe* is pronounced /-ye/ and is written as a suffix added to the noun, for example, آقای نادِری.

The suffix /-ye/ serves other functions as well. When added to names of countries and cities, it denotes where someone is from.

Exercise 25. Listen to the audio and practice the names of countries and nationalities.

Nationality	Country
آلمانی	آلمان
آمریکایی	آمریکا
اِسپانیایی	اِسپانیا
ایتالیایی	ایتالیا
ایرانی	ایران
اَفغانی	اَفغانستان
پاکستانی	پاکستان
ژاپُنی	ژاپُن
فَرانسَوی	فَرانسه
مِصری	مِصر
هِندی	هِند

درس پنج: اهل کجایی؟ Where Are You From?

🎧 **Exercise 26.** Listen to the audio and determine whether the words you hear are countries or nationalities. Make a chart with two categories of countries and nationalities, and then add the words.

Exercise 27. Class Activity.

Write four questions about where your partner and your partner's best friend are from. Then ask the questions and report to the class.

3 Listening and Conversation

Asking Where Someone Is From

There are two ways of asking where someone is from. You may say, "*Shoma kojai hastid?*" (Where are you from?), or "*Shoma ahle kojā hastid?*" (Where are you from?). If the former expression is used, the response is, *man* (nationality) *hastam* (I am . . .), and the proper response for the latter is, *man ahle* (name of country) *hastam*. Depending on the context, responses to both forms may include names of cities, states/provinces, or countries.

اَهلِ کُجایی؟   کُجایی هَستی؟

Exercise 28. Complete the conversations. Then be prepared to hold similar conversations in class with your classmates.

۱. - لیندا اهل آلمانه؟
- نه ، _____ . اون اهل اِنگلیسه.
- شَهرِ لَندَن؟
- آره ، _____ _____ . ولی پدر و مادرِ لیندا اهلِ اِیتالیا _____ .

۲. - تاکاشی ، تو و هاتسوکو _____ ژاپُن هستین؟
- آره ، ما _____ _____ .
- چه خوب! شَهرِ توکیو؟
- مَن _____ توکیو _____ . ولی هاتسوکو _____ _____ .

۳. - دوستهای شما، آرمان و بابَک، _____ اصفهان هستن؟
- نه ، آنها اصفهانی _____ . _____ شیراز هستن.
- شما هم _____ هستین؟
- نه ، من تِهرانی _____ .

درس پنج: اهل کجایی؟ Where Are You From?

Exercise 29. Match the questions with the answers. Then practice with your classmates.

۱. خانواده‌ی شما اهلِ هند هستن؟	الف. بله ، ایشون اهلِ کالیفرنیا هستن.
۲. زَبانِ مادری شما انگلیسیه؟	ب. نه ، نیستن . ایرانی هستن.
۳. تو کانادایی هستی؟	پ. نه، نیست. آلمانیه.
۴. آقای اقبال مصری هستن؟	ت. نه، آنها پاکستانی هستن.
۵. اُستادِ شما اهلِ آمریکاست؟	ج. بله ، من اهلِ کانادا هستم.

🎧 **Exercise 30.**

A. Listen to the audio and practice each line several times. Be prepared to hold a similar conversation in class with your classmates.
B. Listen to the audio and fill in the blanks.

	کِشوَر	شَهر
۱. سینا	....	....
۲. جیمز	....	....

🎧 **Exercise 31.**

A. Listen to the audio and practice each line several times. Be prepared to hold a similar conversation in class with your classmates.
B. Listen to Sara talk to Sophia and her friends. Check True or False.

True	False	
___	___	۱. اینگرید آلمانی است.
___	___	۲. رایان اهل مکزیک است.
___	___	۳. زبانِ کشورِ پاکستان اُردو است.
___	___	۴. سوفیا و ماریا اسپانیایی هستند.

درس پنج: اهل کجایی؟ Where Are You From?

درس پنج: اهل کجایی؟ Where Are You From?

Exercise 32. Class Activity

Dictation: Work with a partner, where one of you will be Student 1 and the other Student 2 giving each other a dictation. Student 1 would be reading List A and Student 2 would be reading List B.

Step 1: Student One covers up List B.
Step 2: Student 1 spells aloud the words from List A for Student 2 to write down.
Step 3: Student 2 writes down the words.
Step 4: Student 2 spells aloud the words from List B as Student 1 writes them down.

List A	List B
کُجایی	اَهلِ
کِشوَر	آمریکا
اِسپانیا	کانادا
اِنگلیس	فَرانسه
اَفغانِستان	پاکِستان
هِند	فَردا
کِلاس	آفتابی
فارسی	اُتاق
کوچَک	بُزُرگ

🎧 **Exercise 33.**

A. Listen to the audio. Practice each line several times and be prepared to hold a similar conversation in class with your classmates.
B. Listen to the audio again and fill in the blanks.

- سلام. صبح بخیر. اسم شما چیه؟
- _____?
- شما اهل _____ ؟
- _____?
- اسم من نازیه. من ایرانیم. شما _____ هستین؟
- من _____ هستم.
- کجای _____ ؟
- نیویورک. _____ من خیلی خوب نیست.
- نه، _____ ! اسم شما چیه؟
- جیمز.
- از دیدن شما خیلی _____ .

Exercise 34. Class Activity.

Go around the room. Ask your classmates and your teacher where they are from. Make a list.

🎧 *Listening and Conversation Vocabulary*

The following is a list of vocabulary terms related to the conversations. The list includes the spoken, as well as the written/formal, form of the vocabulary; their meaning; and their pronunciation using transliteration. The vocabulary terms are organized according to their appearance in the conversations.

Meaning	Transliteration	Written/Formal	Spoken/Colloquial
England	engelis	اِنگلیس	اِینگلیس
Spain	espāniyā	اِسپانیا	اِسپانیا
Mexico	mekzik	مِکزیک	مِکزیک
Urdu	ordu	اُردو	اُردو
How interesting	che jāleb	چه جالِب	چه جالِب

Vocabulary Review Chart

English	Pronunciation	Persian
Sunny	āftābi	آفتابی
Excellent, Bravo	āfarin	آفَرین
German	ālmāni	آلمانی
American	āmrikāi	آمریکایی
Room	otāq	اُتاق
Large, big	bozorg	بُزُرگ
Plate	boshqāb	بُشقاب
Knife	chāqu	چاقو
Doctor	doktor	دُکتُر
Tablecloth	sofre	سُفره
France	fārānse	فَرانسه
Tomorrow	fārdā	فَردا
Rug, carpet	farsh	فَرش
Store	forushgāh	فُروشگاه
Spoon	ghāshoq	قاشُق
Red	qermez	قرمز
Beautiful, pretty	qashang	قَشَنگ
Sugar cube	qand	قَند
Teapot	quri	قوری
Coffee	qahve	قَهوه
Work, job	kār	کار
Employee	kārmand	کارمَند
Book	ketāb	کتاب
Class	kelās	کلاس
Shoe	kafsh	کَفش
Small	kuchak	کوچَک

English	Pronunciation	Persian
Bag, purse	*kif*	کیف
Egypt	*mesr*	مصر
India	*hend*	هِند

Lesson 6

FAMILY

درس شش: خانواده

In this lesson you will learn:

- Letters

  ذ

  ث

- The Silent /vāv/
- Tashdiḍ ّ
- Tanvin ً
- Grammar
  - Pronominal Suffixes
  - The Simple Present Tense
- Listening and Conversation
  - Talking and Asking About Family and Family Relationships

---

1 Letters

A. The Letter (se) ث

The letter *se* is the last of the three letters for the /s/ sound in the Persian alphabet. It is pronounced the same as س and ص, and it generally appears in words of Arabic origin. It is written the same as پ , ب, and ت except that it has three dots above. Like the letters ب ، پ ، ت that you learned in Lesson 1, this letter, too, is a connecting letter. It connects to any letter following it in the initial position. The medial position links it to both preceding and following letters, and in the final position, it connects to a preceding letter.

DOI: 10.4324/9781003223023-6

درس شش: خانواده Family 114

Exercise 1. Watch the video for how the shapes of the letter ث are written. Trace the model letter, and then practice writing your own in the space provided and pronounce it aloud.

B. The Letter (zāl) ذ

The letter *zāl* is the last of the four letters for the sound /z/ in the alphabet. Similar to the letter د, the letter *zāl* has two forms, and connects to any preceding letter if it is not in the freestanding position. It does not connect to a following letter, but unlike د, it has one dot above, as illustrated in the following table.

Connected from the right	Freestanding Position
ـذـ	ذ

Exercise 2. Watch the video for how the shapes of the letter ذ are written. Trace the model letter, and then practice writing your own in the space provided and pronounce it aloud.

Exercise 3. Listen to the following words and repeat.

١. مِثلِ   ٢. مثال   ٣. کاغَذ   ۴. غَذا   ۵. ذُرَت

Exercise 5. Join the letters in each set to form words.

١. م + ِ + ث + ل   ←   ....

٢. غ + َ + ذ + ا   ←   ....

٣. ب + َ + ح + ث   ←   ....

۴. ث + ا + ن + ی + ه   ←   ....

۵. ک + ا + غ + َ + ذ   ←   ....

۶. ذ + ُ + ر + َ + ت   ←   ....

٧. ل + ِ + ذ + َ + ت   ←   ....

٨. ث + ِ + و + ر + َ + ت   ←   ....

٩. م + ُ + ث + ب + َ + ت   ←   ....

١١. آ + ث + ا + ر   ←   ....

١٢. آ + ذ + َ + ر   ←   ....

١٣. م + ُ + ث + َ + ل + َ + ث   ←   ....

١۴. گ + ُ + ذ + َ + ش + ت + ه   ←   ....

Exercise 6. Read the following words. Remember to read from right to left.

١. غَذا   ٢. لَذیذ   ٣. لِذَت

۴. مثلِ   ۵. مُثبَت   ۶. ثروَتمَند

٧. أثر   ٨. آثار   ٩. مِثال

Family خانواده :درس شش

Exercise 7. Write two words for each set of letters.

_____	_____	ث	
_____	_____	س	/s/
_____	_____	ص	
_____	_____	ذ	
_____	_____	ز	/z/
_____	_____	ض	
_____	_____	ظ	

Exercise 8. Practice writing the following words in the space provided.

غَذا غَذا _____

لَذیذ لَذیذ _____

کاغَذ کاغَذ _____

مِثال مِثال _____

مِثل مِثل _____

اَثَر اَثَر _____

🎧 **Exercise 9. Dictation:** Listen to the words dictated to you and write them in the space provided.

۲. _____	۱. _____
۴. _____	۳. _____
۶. _____	۵. _____
۸. _____	۷. _____

C. The Silent /vāv/

In Lesson 2, you learned that when و occurs in the initial and independent positions, it functions as a consonant and is pronounced /v/ as in the word وام and وَ. You also learned that و functions as a vowel in the medial and final positions sounding /u/ as in the word بود.

In this lesson, we focus on the silent *vāv*. In some words of Persian origin, if و is preceded by خ and followed by a long vowel, it becomes silent, as in the words خواهَر /khāhar/ (sister) and خویش /khish/ (self). The origin of these words is Middle Persian. However, they have kept their original orthography in Modern Persian, in particular the combination خوا. Although the very early spelling has been retained, the pronunciation of خوا /khawā/ has changed over the years to خا /khā/ where و is silent.

Exercise 10. Listen to the following words and repeat.

۱. خواهش ۲. خواب ۳. خواهَر
۴. خواندَن ۵. خواستَن ۶. خوابیدَن

درس شش: خانواده Family

Exercise 11. Practice writing the following words in the space provided.

خواهِش خواهِش

خواهَرَم خواهَرَم

خواب خواب

خوابگاه خوابگاه

می خوابَد می خوابَد

می خوانَم می خوانَم

می خواهَم می خواهَم

Exercise 12. Read the following words aloud. Remember to read from right to left.

۱. خواهَرَم ۲. خوابگاه ۳. می خوابَد
۴. می خواهم ۵. می خوابَم ۶. می خوانَم
۷. خواهِش ۸. خواندَن ۹. خوابیدَن

🎧 **Exercise 13. Dictation:** Listen to the words dictated to you and write them in the space provided.

۱. _____ ۲. _____
۳. _____ ۴. _____
۵. _____ ۶. _____
۷. _____ ۸. _____

D. Tashdid ّ

Tashdid (تَشدید) is a diacritical mark used primarily with words of Arabic origin, for example, مُرَبَّع /moraba'/ (square). When a consonant in a syllable is followed by the same exact consonant in the next syllable, *tashdid* is placed above the consonant, and the consonant is written only once. The *tashdid* above the consonant represents 'doubling' of the consonant.

Let's consider the word مُرَبَّع, which has three syllables – مُ - رَب - بَع.) As illustrated in the earlier syllabification, the consonant /ب/ in the second syllable is followed by the same letter in the third syllable. In this 'doubling' of the consonant, the consonant ب is written only once and a *tashdid* is placed above it.

There are not that many Persian words that take *tashdid*. It is important to note that *tashdid* mainly occurs in mid position, as seen in the examples that follow. Also, *tashdid* is commonly omitted in writing by native speakers, although it is sometimes used for clarity.

پ	چ	ر	ک	ل	م
تَپّه	بَچّه	خُرَّم	تِکّه	گَلّه	اُمّید
tappe	bachche	khorram	tekke	galle	ommid
(hill)	(child)	(cheerful)	(piece)	(flock)	(hope)

🎧 **Exercise 14.** Listen to the following words and repeat.

۱. بَچّه   ۲. نَقّاش   ۳. تَشَکُّر

۴. تَوَلُّد   ۵. مُعَلِّم   ۶. مُجَرَّد

🎧 **Exercise 15.** Practice writing the following words in the space provided.

تَوَلُّد تَوَلُّد

تَشَکُّر تَشَکُّر

Exercise 16. Read the following words aloud. Remember to read from right to left.

۱. اَوَّل   ۲. دُوُّم   ۳. سِوُّم
۴. مُعَلِّم   ۵. مُجَرَّد   ۶. تَوَلُّد
۷. نَقّاش   ۸. عَکّاس   ۹. کَفّاش

🎧 **Exercise 17. Dictation:** Listen to the words dictated to you and write them in the space provided.

۱. _____   ۲. _____
۳. _____   ۴. _____
۵. _____   ۶. _____
۷. _____   ۸. _____

E. Tanvin اً

Tanvin, اً, is an adverbial ending that occurs at the end of Arabic loanwords, and it is associated only with the last letter of the word, for example, حَتمَاً /hatman/ (certainly). *Tanvin* is a combination of a short vowel *[a]* and *[n]*, which is pronounced *[an]*, and it consists of an *alef* with two *zebar* (-ً) above it that are found at the end of adverbs of Arabic origin that have kept their original spelling.

It is important to note that Persian words do not take *tanvin*; therefore, words such as ناچاراً *[nāchāran]* (inevitably), should be replaced by به ناچار *[benāchār]* (inevitably), which is a Persian adverb.

Exercise 18. Read the following words aloud. Remember to read from right to left.

۱. اَوَّلاً   ۲. ثانِیاً   ۳. فِعلاً
۴. لُطفاً   ۵. مَعمولاً   ۶. واقِعاً

درس شش: خانواده Family

۷. حَتماً ۸. أصلاً ۹. بَعداً
۱۰. مَثَلاً ۱۱. اِحتمالاً ۱۲. مَخصوصاً

Exercise 19. Practice writing the following words in the space provided.

حَتماً

فِعلاً

لُطفاً

بَعداً

مَثَلاً

واقعاً

مَعمولاً

Exercise 20. You will hear nine words. Circle **a** if you hear a word with *tashdid*, **b** if you hear *tanvin*, or **c** if you hear *kha*.

1. a b c   2. a b c   3. a b c
4. a b c   5. a b c   6. a b c
7. a b c   8. a b c   9. a b c

Exercise 21. Class Activity.
Go around the class and ask six of your classmates to spell their names.

درس شش: خانواده   Family   **122**

Exercise 22. Circle the misspelled word in each set, and write it correctly in the space provided.

	گَذشته	غَذا	خوابگاه
_____	خواهَر	گشنگ	بَچّه
_____	خداحافظ	کلاس	فهلاً
_____	مَثلاً	مُعَلّم	خوانواده

Exercise 23. Make words by completing the following diagram, as in the example.

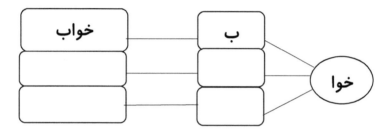

🎧 **Exercise 24. Dictation:** Listen to the words dictated to you and write them in the space provided.

_____ .۲		_____ .۱	
_____ .۴		_____ .۳	
_____ .۶		_____ .۵	
_____ .۸		_____ .۷	
_____ .۱۰		_____ .۹	

Exercise25. Identify ث ذ and the silent *vāv* by circling them in the following:

به نام او که هر چه بخواهد همان است. شبها زود
می خوابم و پیش از خواب «شب به خیر» می گویم.
از خواهرم خواهش کردم برایم کتاب داستان بخواند.
اگر خوب درس بخوانم حتماً قبول می شوم.
از ضَرب المثلهای فارسی
او مدم ثواب کنم کباب شدم
ذَره ذَره جَمع گَردد وانگهی دَریا شَود

2 Grammar

In Lesson 3, you learned about the present tense of the verb "to be" as an irregular verb. In this lesson, you will learn about the pronominal suffixes as well as the simple present tense. The discussion of the simple present tense also includes another irregular verb, "to have".

Pronominal Suffixes

In Lesson 2, you learned about personal pronouns that can function as either the subject or object of the verb. In this lesson, you will learn about a second group of pronouns that consist of suffixes. Pronominal suffixes do not have an independent function and meaning and are connected to other words and are used as possessive pronouns:

مان ⇐ ما		مَ= ⇐ من
تان ⇐ شما		تَ= ⇐ تو
شان ⇐ آنها		شَ= ⇐ او

Pronominal suffixes can connect to nouns, adjectives, or prepositions. When these suffixes are connected to nouns and adjectives and used as possessive pronouns, they function the same as the personal pronouns, as illustrated in the following table.

Noun	مِدادَم ⇐ (مِدادِ من)	/madadam/	my pencil
Adjective	کیفِ کوچَکَت ⇐ (کیفِ کوچَکِ تو)	/kife kochakat/	your small bag
Preposition	بِهِمان ⇐ (به ما)	/beheman/	to us

Exercise 26. Rewrite the following using pronominal suffixes.

۱. خواهَرِ مَن _____
۲. غَذای خوشمَزه ی او _____
۳. خوابگاهِ آنها _____
۴. کتابِ فارسی ما _____
۵. مُعَلِّمِ کلاسِ اَوَّلِ تو _____

The Simple Present Tense

The simple present tense denotes the existence of a state or an event in the present or near future. It can also denote actions that are done habitually. In the formation of the present tense, the prefix می is added to the present stem, and the present stem is added to the verbal ending. It is more common to write the prefix می separately and not connected to the verb.

(They eat in the dorm)	آنها در خوابگاه غَذا می خورَند.
(We are going to Tehran tomorrow)	ما فَردا به تهران می رویم.
(I live in Shiraz)	من در شیراز زندگی می کُنم.
(He/she works everyday)	او هَر روز کار می کُنَد.

Present Stem

In Persian, every verb has a present stem. In order to form a verb in the present tense, knowing the present stem is essential. The present stem of a given verb should be learned along with its infinitive because there is no set formula to obtain the present stem from the infinitive. The infinitive is the basic form of a verb, without an inflection binding it to a particular subject or tense.

Present Stem	Infinitive
خور	خوردَن *khordan* (to eat)
رو	رَفتَن *raftan* (to go)
*کُن	زندگی کردن *zendegi kardan* (to live)

 * **Simple and Compound verbs:** In Persian, a simple verb consists of a one-word infinitive (discussed later), whereas compound verbs have two components, a verb and a nonverbal. In the earlier example, زندگی کردن is a compound verb, consisting of two components, a noun and a simple verb. In the case of compound verbs, only the verb component is conjugated.

The Present-Tense Verbal Endings

The present-tense verbal endings are similar to the short forms of the verb "to be" except for the third-person singular, as shown in the following table.

Plural		Singular	
1st Person	...یم /-im/	1st Person	...َم /-am/
2nd Person (pl)	...ید /-id/	2nd Person	...ی /-i/
3rd Person	...َند /-and/	3rd Person	...َد /ad/

As noted earlier, the present tense is formed by adding the verbal ending to the present stem, which is preceded by the prefix می. In the conjugation of verbs, there has to be agreement between the subject (person and number) and the verb.

Here is an example of the conjugation of the verbs in the simple present tense "to go" (رفتن):

We go	می رویم	I go	می رَوَم
You go (pl)	می روید	You go	می رَوی
They go	می رَوَند	S/he/it goes	می رَوَد

If the present stem ends in ا /ā/ or و /u/, a *ye* is inserted before the verbal ending.

گو	←	گفتَن	آ	←	آمَدَن
		/goftan/			/āmadan/
		(To Say)			(To Come)

Here is the conjugation of آمدن & گفتن in the simple present tense.

می گوییم	می گویَم	می آییم	می آیَم
می گویید	می گویی	می آیید	می آیی
می گویَند	می گویَد	می آیَند	می آیَد

Spoken Form of the Present Tense

The ending of the verbs in third-person singular as well as the second- and third-person plural change in spoken form as follows. Here is an example of the verb "To Have" داشتَن" which is discussed in the next section.

داره	←	دارد
دارین	←	دارید
دارن	←	دارند

The Negation

The negative form of the verbs in the simple present tense is made by adding نـ to the prefix می.

We don't go	نمی رویم	I don't go	نمی رَوَم
You don't go (pl)	نمی روید	You don't go	نمی روی
They don't go	نمی رَوَند	S/he/it doesn't go	نمی رود

The Present Tense of "To Have"

The formation of the simple present tense of "to have" (داشتن) is the same as the other verbs discussed before, except for the addition of the prefix می to the present stem, (دار) Here is the conjugation of داشتن with the present stem (دار)

We have	داریم	I have	دارَم
You have (pl)	دارید	You have	داری
They have	دارَند	He/she has	دارَد

The Negation: The negative form of (داشتن) in the simple present tense is made with adding "نَ" to the present stem. Here are the negative forms of the verb:

We don't have	نداریم	I don' have	نَدارَم
You don't have (pl)	نَدارید	You don't have	نَداری
They don't have	نَدارَند	He/she doesn't have	نَدارَد

Exercise 27. Read the following paragraph. Remember to read from right to left.

اِسم من بیتا است. من بیست سال دارم. دانشجوی دانشگاه تهران هستم.
من در خوابگاهِ دانشجویان زندگی می کنم.
خانواده ی من در تهران زندگی نمی کنند.
آنها در شیراز زندگی می کنند. پِدرم مُهَندِس وَ مادرم مُعَلِّم است.
من یک خواهر و یک برادر دارم.
خواهرم دانشجوی دانشگاه شیراز است. اسم او مینا است. برادرم در بانک کار می کند. اسمِ برادَرم آرَش است. خواهر و برادرم با پدر و مادرم زندگی می کنند.

Exercise 28.

a. Read the paragraph again and complete the sentences.

الف: اسم _____ بیتا _____ .

ب: من _____ سال _____ .

پ: من دانشجوی _____ تهران _____ .

ت: من در _____ دانشجویان زندگی _____ .

ث: خانواده ی من در _____ زندگی _____ .

ج: پدرم _____ و مادرم _____ است.

چ: خواهرم _____ دانشگاه _____ است.

ح: برادرم در _____ کار _____ .

خ: اسم خواهرم _____ و اسم برادرم _____ است.

د: خواهر و _____ با پدر و _____ زندگی _____ .

b. Based on the preceding paragraph, answer the questions.

۱. بیتا چند سال دارد؟ _____

۲. او دانشجوی کجاست؟ _____

۳. خانواده ی بیتا کجا زندگی می کنند؟ _____

۴. او چند خواهر و برادر دارد؟ _____

۵. مادرِ بیتا چه کار می کند؟ _____

Exercise 29. Complete the following paragraph with the appropriate present-tense form of the verbs given.

بیتا یک خواهر و یک برادر _____ (داشتن). او در دانشگاهِ تهران فارسی _____ (خواندن). او بیست سال _____ (داشتن).

خانواده ی او در تهران _____ (زندگی کردن / negative). آنها در شیراز _____ (زندگی کردن). او مَعمولاً در خوابگاه غذا _____ (خوردن). خواهرش شیمی _____ (خواندن) ولی برادرش _____ (درس خواندن / negative). او در بانک _____ (کار کردن). فردا، پدر و مادر بیتا به تهران _____ (آمدن). بیتا خیلی خوشحال _____ (بودن).

Exercise 30. Listen to the pronunciation of the top means of transportation and repeat.

Exercise 31. Listen to the following paragraph and fill in the blanks.

تابستان من و خانواده ام به ایران سَفَر می کنیم. ما با _____ به تهران می رویم. تهران بسیار بُزرگ است. دَر تهران با _____ به هُتلمان می رویم. عَمویم در تهران _____. او به هُتل می آید و با عَمویم _____ بازار می رویم. به

بَعد از چَند روز از تهران با _____ به اصفهان می رَویم. اصفهان خیلی زیبا است. ما در اصفهان _____ به بازار و رستوران می رویم.

خاله ام در اصفهاَن زندگی می کند. او با ما با _____ به شیراز می آید ما دو هَفته در ایران می مانیم.

Exercise 32. Listen to the paragraph again and circle which means of transportation will be used in the trip.

تاکسی	پیاده	کَشتی
دوچَرخه	ماشین	هَواپیما
مِترو	قَطار	موتورسیکلت

Exercise 33. Based on the preceding paragraph, indicate whether each sentence is true or false.

۱. آنها با ماشین به شیراز می رَوند. _____
۲. عمویش در تهران زندگی می کُند. _____
۳. آنها در تابستان سَفَر نمی کنند. _____
۴. آنها با مترو به هُتلشان می رَوند. _____
۵. خاله اش با آنها به شیراز سفر می کُند. _____
۶. آنها با اُتوبوس به اصفهان می رَوند. _____
۷. آنها دو هفته در تِهران می مانند. _____

درس شش: خانواده Family   **131**

3 Listening and Conversation

In this lesson, you learn to talk about your family and relatives as well as ask your classmates about their family.

Exercise 34. Unscramble the questions to complete the following short conversations. After you have completed the conversations, listen to the audio and check your work. Then ask a classmate the questions. Reverse roles and answer with your own information.

۱. - _____ ؟

زندگی / خانواده تون / می کنند / کجا
- تهران. خانواده ام اهل تهران هستند.

۲. - _____ ؟

چطور / شما / خانواده ی
- خانواده ی من شیراز زندگی می کنند.

۳. - _____ ؟

خواهر / دارید / برادر / شما / و
- بله ، یک برادر و یک خواهر دارم.

۴. - _____ ؟

چه / کار / تون / خواهر / می کنند / و / برادر
- هر دو دانشجو هستند.

۵. - _____ ؟

شما / برادر / و / دارید / خواهر
- نه، من خواهر و برادر ندارم.

Exercise 35. Class Activity

Dictation: Work with a partner, where one of you will be Student 1 and the other, Student 2, gives each other a dictation. Student 1 would be reading List A, and Student 2 would be reading List B.

  Step 1: Student 1 covers up List B.
  Step 2: Student 1 spells aloud the words from List A for Student 2 to write down.
  Step 3: Student 2 writes down the words.
  Step 4: Student 2 spells aloud the words from List B as Student 1 writes them down.

درس شش: خانواده Family

List A	List B
معمولاً	مَثَلاً
فِعلاً	حَتماً
خوابگاه	خواهَرم
می خوابم	می خواهد
دوچَرخه	تاکسی
اتوبوس	هَواپیما
مِترو	قَطار
ماشین	موتورسیکلِت

Exercise 37. Complete the sentences about the Tehrani family.

خانواده ی تهرانی

۱. آزاده ـــــــــــــــ اَحمد است.
۲. سینا و بیتا ـــــــــــــــ آنها هستند.
۳. اَحمد ـــــــــــــــ آزاده است.
۴. بیتا ـــــــــــــــ اَحمد است.
۵. سینا ـــــــــــــــ آزاده است.
۶. بیتا ـــــــــــــــ سینا است.
۷. سینا ـــــــــــــــ بیتا است.
۸. اَحمد و آزاده ـــــــــــــــ بیتا و سینا هستند.

درس شش: خانواده Family

🎧 **Exercise 38.** Listen to the audio and complete the chart.

	آشپز	استاد ریاضی	حسابدار	دانشجو	دانش آموز	دکتر	هنرمند
پدرِ							
مادر							
عمو							
خاله							
برادر							
خواهر							
دختر خاله							

🎧 **Exercise 39.**

A. Listen to the audio and practice each line several times. Be prepared to hold a similar conversation in class with your classmates.

B. Listen to the audio again and fill in the blanks.

- شما اهل کجایید؟
- من آبادانیم.
- چه جالب! من آبادان ‎_____.
آبادان چه جور شهریه؟
- گرمه ولی خیلی ‎_____!
من و ‎_____ آبادان زندگی می کنیم ولی ‎_____ تهران زندگی می کنند. ما یک دختر و یک پسر داریم. اونا دانشجو هستن.
- تهران ، کجا زندگی می کنند؟
- دخترم خونه ی ‎_____ زندگی می کنه و پسرم خوابگاهِ ‎_____.
- شما کجایی هستین؟
- من شیرازیم. من و ‎_____ شیراز زندگی می کنیم، و پسرم انگلیس زندگی می کنه. پسرم اونجا درس ‎_____ و دانشگاه هم کار می کنه.
- چه خوب!

Exercise 40. Look at the family tree and complete the sentences.

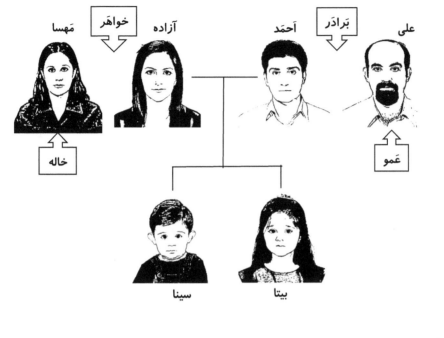

۱. مَهسا ــــــــــــــــــ سینا و بیتا است.
۲. اَحمَد ــــــــــــــــــ علی است.
۳. آزاده ــــــــــــــــــ مهسا است.
۴. علی ــــــــــــــــــ بیتا و سینا است.
۵. مَهسا و علی ــــــــــــــــــ و ــــــــــــــــــ سینا و بیتا هستند.

درس شش: خانواده Family

Exercise 41. Class Activity

In this family tree activity, work with a partner and ask questions about your partner's family members and their relationship to each other. Based on the information, draw your partner's family tree, and then reverse roles.

Exercise 42. Class Activity.

Answer the questions in the chart. Then go around the class and find classmates with the same answers. Write their names in the space provided.

اسم	نَه	بَله	
_____	___	___	۱. با پدر و مادرت زندگی می کنی؟
_____	___	___	۲. پدَر و مادرت کارَ می کنند؟
_____	___	___	۳. شَب ها تِلویزیون تَماشا می کنی؟
_____	___	___	۴. با خانواده شام می خوری؟

🎧 Listening and Conversation Vocabulary

The following is a list of vocabulary terms related to the conversations. The list includes the spoken, as well as the written/formal, form of the vocabulary; their meaning; and their pronunciation using transliteration. The vocabulary terms are organized according to their appearance in the conversations.

Meaning	Transliteration	Written/Formal	Spoken/Colloquial
We travel	safar mikonim	سَفَر می کُنیم	سَفَر می کُنیم
Very	besyār	بسیار	بسیار
After	ba'd az	بَعد از	بَعد از
To	be	به	به
Very	kheyli	خیلی	خیلی
In	dar	دَر	دَر
With	bā	با	با
Week	hafte	هَفته	هَفته
Husband	shohar	شوهَر	شوهَر
Sister	khāhar	خواهَر	خواهَر

Maternal Aunt	khāle	خاله	خاله
What kind	che jur	چه جور	چه جور
It's hot	garme	گرم است	گرمه

Vocabulary Review Chart

English	Pronunciation	Persian
Bus	otobus	اُتوبوس
First	aval	اوّل
Child	bache	بَچّه
On foot	piyāde	پیاده
Taxi	tāksi	تاکسی
Birthday	tavalod	تَولّد
For sure, certainly	hatman	حَتماً
Dormitory	khābgah	خوابگاه
I read	khāndam	خواندم
Request, please	khāhesh	خواهش
Second	dovom	دُوّمِ
Corn	zorat	ذُرّت
Third	sevom	سوّم
Food	ghazā	غَذا
Train	qatār	قَطار
Past	gozashte	گُذشته
Please	lotfan	لُطفاً
Subway	metro	مترو
Such as	mesl	مثلِ
For example	masalan	مَثلاً
Teacher	mo'alem	مُعَلّم
Usually	ma'molan	مَعمولاً
I sleep	mi-khābam	می خوابم
I want	mi-khāham	می خواهم
He/she reads	mi-khānad	می خواند

GLOSSARY

English	Pronunciation	Persian
		الف
Water	āb	آب
Thriving	ābād	آباد
Blue	ābi	آبی
Etiquette	ādāb	آداب
Quiet	ārām	آرام
Flour	ārd	آرد
Yes (informal)	āre	آره
Agency	āzhāns	آژانس
Easy	āsān	آسان
Sky	āsmān, āsemān	آسمان
Pottage	āsh	آش
Cook, chef	āshpaz	آشپز
Familiarity	āshnāi	آشنایی
Sun	āftāb	آفتاب
Bravo, well done	āfarin	آفرین
Mr., Sir	āqā	آقا
Germany	ālmān	آلمان
German	ālmāni	آلمانی
He/She came	āmad	آمَد
To Come	āmadan (ā)	آمَدَن (آ)
America	āmrikā	آمریکا
American	āmrikāi	آمریکایی

English	Pronunciation	Persian
That	ān	آن
Pineapple	ānānās	آناناس
They	ānhā	آنها
Deer	āhu	آهو
Cloud	abr	اَبر
Room	otāq	اُتاق
Bus	otobus	اُتوبوس
Effect(s), work(s)	asar (āsār)	اَثَر (آثار)
Probably	ehtemālan	احتمالاً
News	akhbār	اَخبار
Urdu	ordu	اُردو
From	az	اَز
Horse	asb	اَسب
Spain	espāniyā	اسپانیا
Spanish	espāniyāi	اسپانیایی
Is	ast	اَست
Professor	ostād	اُستاد
Name	esm	اسم
Afghanistan	afghānestān	اَفغانستان
Today	emruz	اِمروز
Finger	angosht	اَنگُشت
England	engelis	انگلیس
English	engelisi	اَنگلیسی
He/she	u	اَو
First	aval	اَوَل
Where are you from	ahl-e kojai	اَهل کُجایی
Italy	itāliyā	ایتالیا
Italian	itāliyāi	ایتالیایی
They (formal)	ishān (ishun)	ایشان (ایشون)
This	in	این
These	inhā	اینها
		ب
With	bā	با
Dad (informal)	bābā	بابا
Wind	bād	باد
Almond	bādām	بادام
Load, time	bār	بار

English	Pronunciation	Persian
Rain	bārān	باران
Open	bāz	باز
Market	bāzār	بازار
Garden	bāgh	باغ
Bank	bānk	بانک
Child	bache	بچه
Discussion	bahs	بحث
Bad	bad	بَد
Brother	barādar	بَرادَر
Snow	barf	بَرف
Rice	berenj	برنج
Big, large	bozorg	بُزُرگ
Very, many	besyār	بسیار
Plate	boshqāb	بُشقاب
Next, then	ba'd	بَعد
After	ba'd az	بَعد از
Later	ba'dan	بَعداً
Nightingale	bolbol	بُلبُل
Ticket	belit	بلیت
Was	bud	بود
To be	budan	بودَن
Spring	bahār	بَهار
Awake	bidār	بیدار
Outside	birun	بیرون
Sick	bimār	بیمار
Nose	bini	بینی
		پ
Foot	pā	پا
Mall	pāsāzh	پاساژ
Passport	pāsport	پاسپورت
Pakistan	pākestān	پاکستان
Fifteen	pānzdah	پانزدَه
Father	pedar	پدَر
Nurse	parastār	پَرَستار
Then, so	pas	پَس
Boy, Son	pesar	پسَر
Bridge	pol	پُل

English	Pronunciation	Persian	
Police	*polis*		پُلیس
Five	*panj*		پَنج
On foot	*piyāde*		پیاده
			ت
Swing	*tāb*		تاب
Summer	*tābestān*		تابستان
History	*tārikh*		تاریخ
Fresh, new	*tāze*		تازه
Taxi	*tāksi*		تاکسی
Bed	*takht*		تَخت
Thanks	*tashakor*		تَشَکُر
Holiday, closed, off	*ta'til*		تَعطیل
Telephone	*telefon*		تِلِفُن
Cell phone	*telefon-e hamrāh*		تِلِفُن هَمراه
To watch	*tamāshā kardan (kon)*		تَماشا کردَن (کُن)
Lazy	*tanbal*		تَنبَل
Fast, spicy	*tond*		تُند
You (singular)	*to*		تو
Ball	*tup*		توپ
Mulberry	*tut*		توت
Birthday	*tavalod*		تَوَلُد
			ث
Fixed	*sābet*		ثابت
Seconds	*sāniye*		ثانیه
Wealth	*servat*		ثِروَت
Rich	*servatmand*		ثِروَتمَند
			ج
Celebration	*jashn*		جَشن
Owl	*joghd*		جُغد
Answer	*javāb*		جَواب
Young	*javān*		جَوان
Scream	*jigh*		جیغ
			چ
Knife	*chāqu*		چاقو
Tea	*chāy*		چای
Why	*cherā*		چرا
Lamp	*cherāgh*		چِراغ

English	Pronunciation	Persian
Eye	cheshm	چشم
How	chetor	چِطور
How are you (informal)	chetori	چِطوری
How are you (pl. formal)	chetorid (chetorin)	چِطورید (چِطورین)
How many, several	chand	چَند
Fork	changāl	چَنگال
Because	chon	چون
What	che (chi)	چه (چی)
How interesting	che jāleb	چه جالِب
What kind	che jur	چه جور
How nice	che khub	چه خوب
Four	chāhār	چَهار
Fourteen	chāhārdah	چَهاردَه
Thing	chiz	چیز
What is it	chist (chiye)	چیست (چیه)
China	chin	چین
		ح
Ready	hāzer	حاضر
Certainly	hatman	حَتماً
Hijab	hejāb	حجاب
Accountant	hesābdār	حَسابدار
Courtyard	hayāt	حَیاط
		خ
Maternal aunt	khāle	خاله
Mrs., madam	khānom (khānum)	خانُم (خانوم)
Family	khānevāde	خانواده
House	khāne	خانَه
News	khabar (akhbār)	خَبَر (اَخبار)
Goodbye	khodāhāfez (khodāfez)	خُداحافظ (خدافظ)
Tired	khaste	خَستَه
Pilot	khalabān	خَلَبان
Sleep	khāb	خواب
Dormitory	khābgāh	خوابگاه
To sleep	khābidan (khāb)	خوابیدَن (خواب)
To want	khāstan (khāh)	خواستَن (خواه)
To read	khāndan (khān)	خواندَن (خوان)
Sister	khāhar	خواهَر

English	Pronunciation	Persian
Request, please	khāhesh	خواهش
Good, fine	khub	خوب
I'm fine	khubam	خوبم
To eat	khordan (khor)	خوردَن (خور)
Sun	khorshid	خورشید
Good	khosh	خوش
Happy	khoshhāl	خوشحال
Delicious	khoshmaze	خوشمَزه
Nice to meet you	khoshvaqtam	خوشوقتَم
Street	khiyābān	خیابان
		د – ذ
He/she gave	dād	داد
He/she has	dārad	دارَد
Pharmacist	dārusāz	داروساز
To have	dāshtan	داشتَن
Wise	dānā	دانا
Knowledge	dānesh	دانش
K–12 student	dāneshāmuz	دانش آموز
College student	dāneshju	دانِشجو
Scientist	dāneshmand	دانِشمَند
Girl	dokhtar	دُختَر
In, at, door	dar	دَر
Tree	derakht	درَخت
To study	dars khāndan (khān)	دَرس خواندَن (خوان)
Sea	daryā	دَریا
Hand	dast	دَست
Notebook	daftar	دَفتَر
Doctor	doktor	دُکتُر
Tooth	dandān	دَندان
World	donyā	دُنیا
Two	do	دو
Twelve	davāzdah	دوازدَه
Bicycle	docharkhe	دوچَرخه
Camera	durbin	دوربین
Friend	dust	دوست
Friendship	dusti	دوستی
I like	dust dāram	دوست دارَم

English	Pronunciation	Persian
Yogurt drink	dugh	دوغ
Second	dovom	دُوم
Ten	dah	دَه
Yesterday	diruz	دیروز
Corn	zorat	ذُرَت
		ر
Radio	rādiyo	رادیو
Satisfied	rāzi	راضی
Related	rabt	رَبط
Restaurant	resturān	رستوران
To go	raftan (rav)	رَفتَن (رَو)
Psychologist	ravānshenās	رَوانشناس
Fox	rubāh	روباه
Day	ruz	روز
Good day	ruz bekheyr	روز بخیر
Math	riyāzi	ریاضی
		ز – ژ
Language, tongue	zabān	زَبان
Time	zamān	زَمان
Winter	zemestān	زَمستان
Woman, wife	zan	زَن
Bee	zanbur	زَنبور
Life	zendegi	زندگی
To live	zendegi kardan (kon)	زندَگی کردَن (کُن)
Very, many, a lot	ziyād	زیاد
Beautiful	zibā	زیبا
Olive	zeytun	زیتون
Japan	zhāpon	ژاپُن
Sweater	zhākat	ژاکت
		س
Clock, hour, time, watch	sā'at	ساعَت
Quiet	sāket	ساکت
Year	sāl	سالَ
Healthy	sālem	سالم
Green	sabz	سَبَز
Vegetables, herbs	sabzi	سَبزی

English	Pronunciation	Persian
Soldier	*sarbāz*	سَرباز
Red	*sorkh*	سُرخ
Travel	*safar*	سَفَر
To travel	*safar kardan (kon)*	سَفَر کردَن (کُن)
Tablecloth	*sofre*	سُفره
White	*sefid*	سفید
Hello	*salām*	سَلام
Health	*salāmati*	سَلامَتی
Whistle	*sut*	سوت
Third	*sevom*	سِوُم
Three	*se*	سه
Black	*siyāh*	سیاه
Apple	*sib*	سیب
Garlic	*sir*	سیر
Thirteen	*sizdah*	سیزدَه
Tray	*sini*	سینی
		ش
Happy	*shād*	شاد
Happiness	*shādi*	شادی
Dinner	*shām*	شام
Sixteen	*shānzdah*	شانزدَه
Night	*shab*	شَب
Good night	*shab bekheyr*	شَب بخیر
Beginning, start	*shoru'*	شُروع
Six	*shesh*	شَش
Poem, poetry	*she'r*	شعر
Job, occupation	*shoghl*	شُغل
Pants	*shalvār*	شَلوار
You (plural)	*shomā*	شُما
Candle	*sham'*	شَمع
Husband	*shohar*	شوهَر
City	*shahr*	شَهر
Lion, milk	*shir*	شیر
Sweet	*shirin*	شیرین
Sweets, pastry	*shirini*	شیرینی
Chemistry	*shimi*	شیمی

English	Pronunciation	Persian
		ص – ض
Soap	*sābun*	صابون
Morning	*sobh*	صُبح
Good morning	*sobh bekheyr*	صُبح بخیر
Breakfast	*sobhāne*	صُبحانه
Talk	*shohbat*	صُحبَت
Sound	*sedā*	صدا
Face	*surat*	صورَت
Pink	*surati*	صورَتی
		ط – ظ
Peacock	*tāvus*	طاووس
Floor	*tabaqe*	طَبقه
Parrot	*tuti*	طوطی
Rope	*tanāb*	طَناب
Noon	*zohr*	ظُهر
		ع – غ
Excellent	*āli*	عالی
Iraq	*arāq*	عَراق
Saudi Arabia	*arabestān*	عَرَبستان
Photographer	*akās*	عَکّاس
Paternal uncle	*amu*	عمو
Paternal aunt	*ame*	عَمه
Celebration	*eyd*	عید
Food	*ghazā*	غَذا
		ف
Persian	*fārsi*	فارسی
Tomorrow	*fardā*	فَردا
Rug	*farsh*	فَرش
Store	*forushgāh*	فُروشگاه
For now, currently	*fe'lan*	فعلاً
Cup	*fenjān*	فَنجان
Soccer	*futbāl*	فَوتبال
		ق
Spoon	*qāshoq*	قاشُق
Rug	*qāli*	قالی
Boat	*qāyeq*	قایق

English	Pronunciation	Persian
Old	*qadimi*	قَدیمی
Red	*qermez*	قرمز
Pretty, beautiful	*qashang*	قَشَنگ
Train	*qatār*	قَطار
Qatar	*qatar*	قَطَر
Sugar cube	*qand*	قَند
Sugar bowl	*qandān*	قَندان
Teapot	*quri*	قوری
Strong	*qavi*	قَوی
Coffee	*qahve*	قَهوه
		ک
Work, job	*kār*	کار
To work	*kār kardan (kon)*	کار کردَن (کُن)
Computer	*kāmputer*	کامپیوتر
Employee	*kārmand*	کارمَند
Paper	*kāghaz*	کاغَذ
Canada	*kānādā*	کانادا
Kabab	*kabāb*	کباب
Coat, jacket	*kot*	کُت
Book	*ketāb*	کتاب
Where	*kojā*	کُجا
Ship	*kashti*	کشتی
Country	*keshvar*	کشوَر
Shoemaker	*kafāsh*	کَفاش
Shoe	*kafsh*	کفش
Classroom	*kelās*	کلاس
Small, little	*kuchak*	کوچَک
Bag	*kif*	کیف
Cake	*keyk*	کیک
		گ
Cow	*gāv*	گاو
Past	*gozashte*	گُذَشته
Cat	*gorbe*	گُربه
Walnut	*gerdu*	گردو
Warm	*garm*	گَرم
To say, to tell	*goftan (gu)*	گُفتَن (گو)

English	Pronunciation	Persian
Flower	gol	گُل
Ear	gush	گوش
Meat	gusht	گوشت
Cherry	gilās	گیلاس
		ل
Lip	lab	لَب
Clothes	lebās	لباس
Smile	labkhand	لَبخَند
Pleasure, joy	lezat	لذَت
Delicious	laziz	لَذیذ
		م
We	mā	ما
Mother	mādar	مادَر
Snake	mār	مار
Yogurt	māst	ماست
Car	māshin	ماشین
Mom	māmān	مامان
To stay	māndan (mān)	ماندَن (مان)
Fish	māhi	ماهی
Translator	motarjem	مُتَرجِم
Subway	metro	مترو
Thank you	motshakeram	مُتشَکِرَم
Example	mesāl	مثال
Positive	mosbat	مُثبَت
Such as, like	mesl-e	مثل
Triangle	mosalas	مُثَلَث
For example	masalan	مَثلاً
Single	mojarad	مُجَرَد
Environment	mohit	مُحیط
Special	makhsus	مَخصوص
Especially	makhsusan	مَخصوصاً
Pencil	medād	مداد
School	madrese	مَدرسه
Related	marbut	مَربوط
Man	mard	مَرد
Thank you	mersi	مرسی
Chicken	morgh	مُرغ
Duck	morghābi	مُرغابی

English	Pronunciation	Persian	
Sick	*mariz*		مَریض
Homework	*mashq*		مَشق
East	*masherq*		مَشرق
Egypt	*mesr*		مصر
Introduction	*mo'arefi*		مُعَرفی
Teacher	*mo'alem*		مُعَلم
Usually	*ma'mulan*		مَعمولاً
Meaning	*ma'ni*		مَعنی
Thank you	*mamnun*		مَمنون
I	*man*		مَن
Waiting	*montazer*		مُنتَظِر
Me too	*manam hamintor*		مَنَم هَمینطور
Careful	*movāzeb*		مُواظِب
Motorcycle	*motorsiklet*		موتورسیکلِت
Banana	*moz*		موز
Mouse	*mush*		موش
Subject, topic	*mozu'*		موضوع
Kind	*mehrabān*		مهرَبان
Guest	*mehmān*		مهمان
Engineer	*mohandes*		مُهَندِس
I Come	*mi-āyam*		می آیَم
He/she sleeps	*mi-khābad*		می خوابَد
I read	*mi-khānam*		می خوانَم
I want	*mi-khāham*		می خواهَم
I go	*mi-ravam*		می رَوَم
Desk	*miz*		میز
We stay	*mi-mānim*		می مانیم
			ن - و
Orange	*nārenji*		نارنجی
Name	*nām*		نامَ
Letter	*nāme*		نامه
Bread	*nān*		نان
He/she does not have	*nadārad*		نَدارَد
Nowruz	*noruz*		نوروز
Opinion, look	*nazar*		نَظَر
Painter	*nāqāsh*		نَقاش
Nineteen	*nuzdah*		نوزده
Writer	*nevisande*		نِویسَنده

English	Pronunciation	Persian	
No	na		نَه
Nine	noh		نُه
Is not	nist		نیست
I am not	nistam		نیستَم
You are not (sing.)	nisti		نیستی
Also	niz		نیز
Volleyball	vālibāl		والیبال
But	vali		وَلی
			ه
Hotel	hotel		هُتل
Eighteen	hejdah		هَجدَه
Is	hast		هَست
I am	hastam		هَستَم
You are (sing.)	hasti		هَستی
Eight	hasht		هَشت
Seven	haft		هَفت
Week	hafte		هَفته
Seventeen	hefdah		هفدَه
Also	ham		هَم
All	hame		هَمه
India	hend		هند
Art	honar		هُنَر
Artist	honarmand		هُنَرمَند
Air, weather	havā		هَوا
Airplane	havāpeymā		هَواپیما
			ی
Or	yā		یا
Memory	yād		یاد
Help	yāri		یاری
Eleven	yāzdah		یازدَه
Jasmine	yās		یاس
It means	ya'ni		یَعنی
One	yek		یک
Greece	yunān		یَونان

Milton Keynes UK
Ingram Content Group UK Ltd.
UKHW032242081223
434061UK00008B/64